German Jews

German Jews

A Dual Identity

PAUL MENDES-FLOHR

Yale University Press　New Haven & London

Designed by James J. Johnson and set in Trump type by Tseng Information Systems, Inc..
Printed in the United States of America by Vail-Ballou Press, Binghamton, New York.

The paper in this book meets the guidelines for permanence and durability of the Committee on Production Guidelines for Book Longevity of the Council on Library Resources.

10 9 8 7 6 5 4 3 2 1

Library of Congress
Cataloging-in-Publication Data

Mendes-Flohr, Paul R.
German Jews : a dual identity /
Paul Mendes-Flohr.
p. cm.

Includes bibliographical references and index.
ISBN 0-300-07623-1 (alk. paper)

1. Jews—Germany—Identity.
2. Jews—Cultural assimilation—Germany. 3. Rosenzweig, Franz, 1886–1929. 4. Germany—Ethnic relations. I. Title.
DS135.G33M48   1999
305.8924'043—dc21   98-32151

A catalogue record for this book is available from the British Library.

I have never had the need to simplify myself or to create an artificial unity through denial; I accept my complexity and hope to be even more many-sided than I am now aware of.

GUSTAV LANDAUER
"Are These Heretical Thoughts?" (1913)

Contents

Preface

Aside from Chapter 1 and the Epilogue, this volume is based on the Franz Rosenzweig Lectures in Jewish Theology and History that I delivered at Yale University in April 1991. Sponsored by the Estate of the late Arthur A. Cohen, the lectures were an occasion to pay homage to two stellar figures who have played an immeasurable role in my life, Arthur Cohen and Franz Rosenzweig. Arthur — or Aharon, as he liked me to call him in Hebrew — was a dear friend and an ever gracious, supportive colleague. And Franz Rosenzweig has been for me an enduring source of spiritual and intellectual inspiration ever since I was a graduate student under the tutelage of the late Nahum N. Glatzer.

I met Arthur through the concatenations of circumstance and chance, although in retrospect it seems that we were destined to meet — as perhaps is true for all genuine friendships. My acquaintance with Rosenzweig was determined by the curriculum required of all students of modern Jewish thought. In my initial engagement with his writings, I was privileged to have Glatzer as my guide; he had been a close associate of Rosenzweig's in Germany and his preeminent interpreter in the United States.

Yet it is not the fortuity of my biography that links Arthur and Rosenzweig. Arthur was profoundly drawn to

Rosenzweig, undoubtedly discerning in the great German-
Jewish philosopher the intense spirituality and theological earnestness of a kindred soul. It was as a pub-
lisher that Arthur was responsible for making available
to English-language readers two of Rosenzweig's most important writings. In the early 1950s Arthur commissioned
a translation of Rosenzweig's *Understanding the Sick and
Healthy* (with an introduction by Nahum Glatzer), which
was issued under the imprint of Noonday Press, of which
Arthur was the founding president. In the early 1960s it
was Arthur, then vice-president of the publishing house of
Holt, Rinehart, and Winston, who supervised the publication of Rosenzweig's magnum opus, *The Star of Redemption*, deftly and devotedly translated by William Hallo of
Yale University.

Among the major projects that Arthur never completed
owing to his untimely death was a detailed commentary
on *The Star*, which, as he envisioned it, would serve as a
sort of Rashi for Rosenzweig's often exasperatingly arcane
philosophical and theological disquisition. He left volumi-
nous notes and drafts of various chapters, now deposited
at Yale. Also available are tapes of a seminar that Arthur
gave at Columbia University, a seminar that allowed him
to test various exegetical strategies for decoding *The Star*.
It is hoped that one day an industrious scholar will make
some of this splendid material accessible to us.

The thematic thrust of this volume was inspired by
Rosenzweig. In the translation of the Hebrew Scripture
into German that he undertook with Martin Buber, he suggested that the Hebrew term Naharayim in Genesis 24:
10, usually translated as Mesopotamia (e.g., by Luther) or
Babylonia, be rendered literally, as *Zweistromland*, "land
of two rivers." Rosenzweig employed the term metaphori-

cally when he used it for the title of his 1926 collection of
essays on Jewish and general cultural topics. Rosenzweig
meant to underscore, indeed, to celebrate, the fact that the
German-Jewish reality is fed, nurtured, by two sources:
German culture and the Jewish religious and spiritual heritage. In this volume I endeavor to explore through the
prism of Rosenzweig's image how German Jews understood and contended with their twofold spiritual patrimony. I trust I have done so in a way that would resonate
with Arthur's thoughts on the subject.

In 1983 Arthur published a novel, *An Admirable
Woman*, that critics sought to read as a roman à clef, identifying its protagonist as Hannah Arendt. Arthur vigorously
protested. I accept his demurral. But perhaps the true protagonist was not a particular person but the German Jew
personified as Arthur's admired woman. Although he himself was of Russian-Jewish origin, he was deeply fascinated
by the German Jew. I surmise that he offers the novel as
an appraisal of the experience of German Jewry, which in
so many ways is paradigmatic for the Jewish experience of
the modern world. The novel opens with the following observations: "I am not wholly admirable. I admit this without embarrassment, even though the Chancellor of my
university, reporting what he had told his trustees when I
was appointed, had said I was 'wholly admirable.' In this
country [the United States] hyperbole is a way of life. The
truth is that in some respects, I am admirable and for the
rest quite unexceptional. . . . Whatever my personality—
its stubbornness, its pleasure in combat, its intolerance
of stupidity—it is my *brain*, not my personality, that is
unconditionally admired. It is treated like an organ in for-
maldehyde, stripped of the animate life of affections and
passions, which, after all, charge the brain and impel its

course. Those who would treat my brain as though it were not party to my passions lie about me more deeply than those who deny I have a brain at all."

Heeding Arthur's sapient counsel, I have sought in this volume to understand the intellectual and cultural achievements of German Jewry within the context of its "animate life of affections and passions."

Acknowledgments

This book was born out of a conversation reaching back to my youth—a conversation conducted as much on street corners as in the corridors of the university; indeed, its most important moments were in coffee shops and under umbrellas while waiting for a bus on rainy days. The partners in this rambling and ongoing conversation are innumerable; many I have undoubtedly forgotten, and others, I fear, were imaginary (even when a specific person stood before me). Nonetheless, there are individuals whose names I wish to recall here, if only to express my affectionate gratitude to them for listening to me and allowing me to listen to them.

The problematic of living with multiple identities first gained articulate expression for me through my friendship with Arnie Schwartz, who at thirteen enthralled me with his precocious poetry and wit. Beginning in summer camp and continuing in the banana groves of Kibbutz Gesher Haziv and the cafes of Greenwich Village, in the graduate seminars at Brandeis University, where we were students together, and finally back in Israel, we traversed a long road together, literally and spiritually. Arnie was my soundest guide and most intimate and understanding friend. He died of a cerebral embolism at the age of forty-seven. The dedication of this book to his memory marks a void, across which I can but utter, "Thanks, Arnie!"

Other vintage friends who have shared in the conversation that informs this book are Gordon Fellman, Michael Fishbane, Susan Jacoby, Jeffrey Jampel, Philip Lamb, Alex Liazos, Galit Hasan-Rokem and Freddie Rokem, and Stefan Rothschild. (I am certain I have forgotten someone. I beg his or her forgiveness.) Others joined the conversation later but no less decisively. Henry Abramovitch, Mohammed Abu-Zaid, Janet Aviad, Celia Brickman, Menachem Brinker, the late Arthur Cohen, Wendy Doniger, Jerold Frakes, Zeev Gries, Samuel Jaffee, Rita Mendes-Flohr, Gabriel Motzkin, Nathan Offek, the late Gillian Rose, the late Nathan Rotenstreich, Eric Santner, Avraham (Patchi) Shapira, Anthony Skinner, Gary Smith, Greg Spinner, and Martina Urban have, each in their own inimitable way, plugged into my struggle with the issues addressed in this volume. My conversations with Martina were seminal for the arguments advanced in the introductory chapter. Many of the insights—and, indeed, guiding perspectives—articulated here gained an existential clarity through my friendship with Martina, for which I must record a special note of gratitude.

To be sure, the conversations leading to this book did not always directly or explicitly touch upon its theme; more often than not, the conversations were conducted semiotically, through gestures, groans, laughter, and tears in visceral response to matters pertaining to our fractured existence as participants in a plurality of cultural discourses and communities of sentiment. Such is the grammar of true conversation. I thus gratefully dedicate this volume to my *Gesprächspartner*, my friends.

In 1969 I made my first visit to Germany. I did so with great trepidation and a measure of guilt, or rather an uneasy feeling that I was trespassing on forbidden terrain, that I entered a territory placed off limits by Jewish memory. I still live with this feeling, and yet I have learned to recognize that memory, as one of the wellsprings of identity, dwells in the protean reality of the here and now and thus in ever changing social and political (as well as emotional) realities. Similarly, as an aspect of one's identity, intercultural discourse, which takes place within oneself as much as between oneself and others, goes back and forth between the liminal regions of time and space. This I have learned from Klaus Affeld, whom I met soon after I arrived in Berlin. I rented a room in the *Wohngemeinschaft* (commune) organized by Klaus. We immediately became fast friends. We have rarely spoken directly about Germans and Jews or the Shoah (Holocaust)—not that we denied or ignored these matters. On the contrary. Klaus never denied being a German or bearing the burdens of his past as a German, nor did I dissimulate my Jewishness. Our identities and memories as a German and a Jew, respectively, were woven into the very fabric of our relationship, and we built upon them naturally as our friendship grew—and continues to grow.

During my visit to Yale University, when I delivered the lectures upon which this book is based, I was graciously hosted by Paula Hyman. Geoffrey Hartman and his wife, Renée, were also kind and solicitous hosts. My student Benjamin Pollack read the penultimate draft of this study and with a disarming gentleness raised issues challenging me to clarify and fine-tune my argument. In addition, I wish to thank Charles Grench, editor in chief at Yale University Press. He not only evinced from the very start encouraging interest in this volume but manifested extraordinary forbearance while awaiting completion of its inordinate period of gestation. I trust he will note that his initial editorial suggestions were not ignored. Mary Pasti edited the manuscript and oversaw its production with exemplary care and judgment. I thank Richard Miller and Ashraf Noor for their conscientious proofreading, sparing me many embarrassments. I am likewise profoundly grateful to Otto Bohlmann, assistant acquisitions editor, as well as everyone else at Yale University Press who took part in seeing this volume to press.

German Jews

Chapter One

The Bifurcated Soul of the German Jew

History, according to Heinrich Heine, is to be told by poets, not historians. A people "demands its history from the hand of the poet rather than that of the historian. It does not ask for faithful reporting of naked facts; what it wants is to see these dissolved again into the original poetry from which they sprang."[1] Commanding access to the memories and lived experiences of a people, the poet tells the people's story.

In a passage of a novella entitled *Leaves from the Memoirs of Herr von Schnabelewopski* (1834),[2] a parody on German student life and German nobility, Heine includes a vignette that poignantly, if somewhat melodramatically, captures the tragic predicament of German Jewry as they sought to maintain a loyalty to their ancestral patrimony while embracing the modern world.[3] Simson, a Jewish student, valiantly defends the biblical conception of God in the face of the cynical agnosticism of the day. His pride leads to a duel with a freethinker. Feeble and small in stature, he is easily overcome by his opponent, who plunges his sword through Simson's lung. On his deathbed, Simson requests that he be read the passage from the Bible regarding his namesake, Samson (Book of Judges 13–16). As he listens to the tale of the cruel treatment of the ancient Israelites at the hands of the Philistines, Simson, free associating, mumbles recollections of the many humiliations suffered by German Jewry. When the reader comes to the scriptural passage in which Samson, betrayed and blinded, defiantly says, "Let my soul die with the Philistines," and pulls the pillars of their temple down upon himself and his tormentors, "little Samson [Simson] opened his eyes uncannily wide, raised himself convulsively, grasped the two pillars at the foot of the bed and shook them, stammering angrily: 'Let my soul die with the Philistines.' But the strong pillars of his bed remained immovable; exhausted, the little man fell back on his pillows with a melancholy smile, and from his wound . . . a red stream of blood oozed out."[4] Simson's melancholic grin—shielding a defiant, paroxysmatic pride—would haunt German Jewry and, indeed, may be seen as a foreboding of the catastrophe that befell it a hundred years after Heine penned his novella.

To reflect on the experience of German Jewry is difficult without a poet's attention to the painful experiences that shaped its grim and ultimately apocalyptic reality. The Holocaust casts a dark shadow on German-Jewish history. Yet surveying that history from this perspective alone may becloud our appreciation of the nuanced terrain traveled by German Jews since Moses Mendelssohn (1729–1786) took the first steps beyond the ghetto walls to join enlightened Germans in the pursuit of shared human concerns. Enlightened culture—guided by the ethic of *Bildung* (the educational ideal of self-cultivation)—inspired German Jewry to the very end.[5] As Heine's tale of the "tragic-comic" death of Simson attests, German Jewry was hardly naive about the social and political obstacles it faced. The view that German Jewry was benighted, beguiled by an imagined but nonexistent symbiosis between Judaism and German culture,[6] is an ahistorical construction—a summary judgment perhaps inevitably dictated by the trajectory from assimilation to Auschwitz that tragically sets the narrative coordinates of German-Jewish history.[7]

German Jews, however, were painfully aware, as the liberal rabbi Benno Jacob put it in 1927, that they were but "assimilated in the accusative"—that is, they assimilated the cultural values of Germany—and not "assimilated in the dative," that is, they were not assimilated into German society.[8] They remained by and large socially apart; hence, their assimilation was never as complete or absolute as is commonly believed. Assimilation—"acculturation" is undoubtedly a better term[9]—was a highly differentiated process in which Jewish identity, knowledge, and commitment were maintained in varying degrees.[10] Acculturation thus cannot be facilely equated with an abandonment of Judaism. But by virtue of the adoption of *Kultur* and Bildung—grounded in the cultivation of universal values sponsored by enlightened, liberal German discourse —German Jews were no longer simply or unambiguously Jewish. Their identity and cultural loyalties were fractured, and they were consequently obliged to confront the challenge of living with plural identities and cultural affiliations. An explication of how they perceived this challenge is the focus of this volume.

German Jewry has been referred to as a "mirror of modernity." Gerson D. Cohen, who coined this apt phrase, had the specifically Jewish experience of the modern world in mind: "It was German Jewry that provided Jews everywhere with mature alternative models of Jewish response to modernity, from radical assimilation to militant Zionism and neo-orthodoxy, as well as a fresh rediscovery of the Jewish past and reformulation of Jewish identity and commitment."[11] I would add that German Jewry's articulate struggle to live with a plurality of identities and cultures— which is increasingly recognized to be a salient feature of

Western modernity—is a mirror of a larger phenomenon beyond the specifics of Jewish existence.[12]

In a comparative study of the construction of modern French and German identities, the anthropologist Louis Dumont contends that members of traditional or premodern societies "know that their personal identity is inseparable from a collective identity."[13] In contradistinction to a traditional or "holistic" configuration of identity, Dumont notes that modern "individualism" regards personal identity as autonomous and primary, and collective identities as "accidental" and "non-essential."[14] In actuality, Dumont holds, these two types of identity formation overlap, often abiding in dialectical tension with one another. "In general, [individualism] applies selectively to some domains of social life—first of all the political—while it accommodates to what is there, or combines with an attachment to tradition, in other domains."[15] In nineteenth-century Germany, Dumont argues, the resulting tension found expression in competing models of collective identity, which alternatively gave primacy to either holistic or individualistic impulses. The holistic alternative was grounded in the notion of *Volk*, the primordial community of the Germanic peoples. The individualistic model derived its principal inspiration from the Enlightenment and was fashioned according to the values of Bildung.

A territorial[16] or a political coding of a German identity was foreclosed by the fact that Germany only became a nation-state under Bismarck's leadership in 1871;[17] prior to the establishment of the Second Reich, Germany was a bewildering array of independent principalities and states.[18] Within the political tapestry of Europe, Germany was a "belated nation," to use the words of Helmut Plessner.[19] Eighteenth- and nineteenth-century votaries of a unified German identity were thus obliged to appeal to either ethnic or cultural criteria.[20] Indeed, prior to Bismarck's state, Germans regarded themselves as either a *Kulturnation* or simply a transterritorial Volk. Sensing themselves excluded by the latter conception of a German identity, Jews were naturally drawn to a cultural coding of *Deutschtum*.[21] As I discuss in Chapter 2, Jews embraced the ethic of Bildung with a single-minded devotion. They were "Germans by the grace of Goethe" *(Deutsche von Goethes Gnaden)*.[22] This quip, which became part of German-Jewish folklore, had an ironic edge, however.

Within the context of their struggle for emancipation, the German Jews' romance with Bildung took on an unanticipated and ultimately deeply troubling dialectical spin. With the first breach of medieval restrictions that kept them a "people apart," Jews rushed to join the so-called *Bildungsbürgertum*, or the educated middle classes. This uniquely German notion and its application to the situation of German Jewry deserves some analysis. In a strict sociological sense, the term refers to a rather small stratum of German society that earned its status by virtue of educational attainments.[23] But since the early nineteenth century the German middle classes had already self-consciously identified with the values of Bildung. The Bildungsbürgertum thus included consumers as well as producers of Bildung and Kultur.[24] Middle-class Jews became conspicuous supporters of high culture. They filled the concert halls and theatres, purchased art, assembled home libraries honoring the canon of educated Germany, and provided their children with the finest humanistic education.

Anecdotal—and statistical—illustrations testifying to the Jews' cultural embourgeoisement abound; some of them lace the text of this volume.[25] They point not only to the fervent participation of Jews in the culture of Bildung but also to what was widely perceived to be their hugely disproportionate numbers within the ranks of the Bildungsbürgertum. Here I shall cite one further witness to this phenomenon, which, for many Germans, was jarring, if not also profoundly disturbing. The poet and novelist Theodor Fontane (1819–1898) penned a poem on the occasion of his seventy-fifth birthday recording his grateful acknowledgment of the many laudations he had received. The poem, perhaps his most famous, alludes to Fontane's numerous writings in celebration of the heroic history and landscape of Germany: the four-volume *Wanderungen durch die Mark Brandenburg* (Ramblings through the Mark of Brandenburg), which appeared between 1862 and 1882.

On My Seventy-fifth Birthday

A hundred letters arrived.
I was dazed with joy,
Puzzled only by the names
And by the places from which they came.

Lulled by vanity, I thought:
You are the man of the *Wanderungen*,
You are the man of the poems on the Mark [of
    Brandenburg],
You are the man of the history of the Mark,
You are the man of old Fritz [Frederick the Great]
And of those who sit with him at the table,
Some chatting, others mute,
First in Sanssouci, then in Elysium.
You are the man of the Prussian aristocracy:
Jagow and Lochow,

Stechow and Bredow, Quitzow and Rochow.
You know no greater merit
Than that of the towns of Schwerin and old Zieten.
You found in all the world nothing to praise
As much as Oppen and Groeben and Kracht and
    Thümen;
In the battles [of Prussia that I have described] and
    at the peak of my enthusiasm
Marched the Pfuels and Itzenplitze,
And from Uckermark, Havelland, and Barnim
Marched the Ribbecks and Kattes, the Bülows and
    the Arnims,
Marched the Treskows and Schlieffens and
    Schliebens—
And about all of them I have written.

But those who came to my day of celebration,
Had very, very different names,
And *sans peur et reproche,* "without fear and
    blame,"
Almost all came from prehistoric nobility:
Names with "berg" and "heim" are not at all to be
    found among them.
They storm in, in their masses:
Meyers come in battalions,
Also Pollacks and those who reside even further
    east,
Abram, Isaac, Israel—
All the patriarchs are on hand.
They place me cordially at their head.
. . . .
For each I have meant something.
All have read me,

All have long known me,
And this is the main thing . . . ,
"Come on, Cohen."[26]

Fontane's ironic acceptance of the Jews' adoration high-
lights their separateness: despite their Bildung they were
still seen as a group apart. They, of course, did not need
Fontane to remind them of that. In 1894, when he wrote his
poem, political and racial antisemitism in Germany had
become particularly virulent.[27] Jews had, however, come
to regard liberal intellectuals like Fontane as their allies.
Since the beginning of their struggle for civic equality—the
so-called movement for Jewish Emancipation—this alli-
ance with the liberal, educated strata of German society
was sealed in the common pursuit of Bildung and Kultur.

Bildung, in its initial articulation, was grounded in a
vision of a "neutral society," a cultural and thus social space
in which matters of primordial and religious background
were regarded as utterly irrelevant to one's qualifications
to enter that space.[28] In principle, Bildung and its supporting social structures were open to one and all. But the open,
tolerant, neutral character of this society was soon threatened and then severely undermined.[29] Social and political
forces conspired to constrict the neutral, open character
of the social structures engendered by the ethos of Bildung.[30] The educated were conscripted into the service of
the evolving state bureaucracies, and the horizons of Bildung were increasingly delimited by parochial (national)
considerations. The respectability and social status at-
tached to Bildung, as George Mosse observes, "soon became a monopoly of a caste rather than accessible to
anyone willing and able to participate in the process of self-
cultivation."[31] In a masterly study—*Arbeit am nationalen
Gedächtnis* (Work on national memory)—Aleida Assmann

amplifies Mosse's observation, illuminating it with the
inner logic of Bildung, especially as Bildung was drawn into
the complex, protracted process of constructing a compelling collective identity for Germans.[32]

Assmann notes that the career of Bildung in Germany
had two separate vectors. One had a formal cultural-
epistemological thrust, and the other a social-political one.
Although the two were destined to overlap and, in some
respects, merge, Assmann argues that the distinctive dynamic of each should be carefully delineated should we
wish to understand how Bildung, which emerged as an
inclusive, cosmopolitan ethos, became not only socially
privileged but also increasingly nationalized and exclu-
sive. As a result of the dual thrust, we find the Jews be-
twixt and between, as Mosse and others have pointed out.
Having ventured on the path of modernity by following the
vision of a neutral society, they adopted a liberal, cosmopolitan conception of Bildung, assuming that it would lead
to their acceptance in and integration into a new social
and political order; but as Germany abandoned that ideal
they often found themselves virtually alone.[33] Assmann's
analysis adds important nuance and allows us to view the
ultimate isolation of the Jewish Bildungsbürgertum in a
larger context and not only in terms of intractable preju-
dices toward them or in terms of the political and moral
faults of the Germans. She addresses the issue from the
perspective of our question of how a national community
can maintain a collective identity that is not only not ex-
clusive but also open, tolerant, and pluralistic.[34]

The career of Bildung as traced by Assmann along its
cultural-epistemological vector is particularly illuminating for our study. Assmann begins her narrative with the
philosopher J. G. Herder (1744–1803), noting that he was
among the first to reflect systematically on the concept of

Bildung, which he pointedly distinguished from the classical ideal of encyclopedic erudition *(Gelehrsamkeit).*[35] Whereas the latter was marked by mastery of a given, fixed body of knowledge, Bildung was driven by an unending exploration of new, ever unfolding vistas of knowledge and, one must add, aesthetic experience. Whereas the old scholastic learning was grounded in a knowledge of an ancient, sacred language, namely Latin, the new learning was conducted in the vernacular of the day.

Bildung had roots in the classical Greek notion of education, *paedeia*—or *humanitas,* as Varro and Cicero translated it—and thus had an emphasis on the nurturing of one's inner life and development, an emphasis reinforced by medieval Christian concepts of education. In consonance with this conception of education and culture as preeminently spiritual activities, Herder took Bildung one crucial step past the Enlightenment conception of education—especially its French version, which adhered to what the late Hans Blumenberg aptly called the "eschatology of the book."[36] Bildung, Herder averred, has no *eschaton,* no end other than itself; it is an eternal, unending process; its goal is self-refinement and the enhancement of one's humanity through a continuously deepening knowledge of the world.[37] Accordingly, Wilhelm von Humboldt (1767–1835) contrasted Bildung with Civilization.[38] Serving no instrumental goal, either pragmatic or ideological, and inspired by a passionate commitment to inner growth and to truth, Bildung has often been characterized as a secular religion.[39] I might parenthetically speculate that it was because of its noninstrumental religious character that former students of the yeshivah (Talmudic academy) felt an immediate affinity with its animating ethos. But Bildung was not only a secular religion; it was also emphatically humanistic. Under the aegis of the Enlightenment, huma-

nitas was not just an educational and anthropological concept but also an ethical ideal: All human beings, irrespec-
tive of cultural and religious background, ultimately form
one family. All of human experience is relevant to one's
self-understanding and hence personal dignity. The ambit
of knowledge is universal.

Associated with a vernacular language, Bildung took on
a national character—German—that from the very start
placed strains on its cosmopolitan scope.[40] This paradoxi-
cal situation became manifest when the Bavarian minister of education F. J. Niethammer turned to Goethe in
1808 and requested his assistance in preparing a textbook
—Nationalbuch—to promote the general education (Bildung) of the German people.[41] Niethammer argued that
the task was especially urgent because the Germans, unlike the French and other peoples of Europe, lacked territorial unity and a common political identity. A Nationalbuch would provide "a unifying point for the education of
all sectors of [German] society."[42] So began the quest for a
national canon that would furnish a cultural—as opposed
to the evasive political or territorial—coding of a German
collective identity.[43] In the wake of the quest, Germans—
at least those associated with the humanistic ideal of Bildung—were wont to speak of themselves as members of a
Kulturnation.[44] It was at this juncture that the ideal of Bildung was conscripted by the politics of identity.

The Nationalbuch contemplated by Niethammer was
perpetually postponed, although an informal German cultural canon eventually did crystallize, including as its cen-
terpiece the writings of Goethe.[45] The recurrent deferment
of the project was probably due not only to the inherent
difficulty of agreeing upon a canon but also to the innate
contradiction of the very idea of a canon to the character of Bildung as a plastic, dynamic conception of culture

and learning. Clearly, Bildung *eo ipso* is antagonistic to a closed, authoritative conception of a canon. A consistent conception of Bildung also seems inevitably to resist the normative conception of a culture implicit in the demand for a canon. In Neitzsche's famous excoriation of the German bourgeoisie and their superficial—Philistine, as he put it—abuses of Bildung, the philosopher also pointed to the expansive, centrifugal nature of humanistic knowledge as inexorably leading to a syncretistic confounding of all values. The Bildungsbürgertum, in the insatiable search for new knowledge, Nietzsche observed, crossed erstwhile boundaries to reach ever broadening cultural horizons, yet a critical historical consciousness weakens the axiological ground of one's primordial culture.[46] The resulting cultural relativism begets what Wilhelm Dilthey later called an "anarchy of values."[47] As a cure for this "unpatriotic learning" *(unnationale Gebildetheit)*, Nietzsche unabashedly recommended replacing Bildung, with its cosmopolitan thrust, with "a true German Bildung."[48] The new cultural and educational ideal was furthered by what he and Richard Wagner ceremoniously called "the rebirth of German myth."[49] When this program was adopted by those bent on an ethnic, not to speak of a racial, coding of German identity, the ideal of Bildung was utterly vitiated, if not fatally compromised.

The one group not to compromise the liberal, cosmopolitan image of Bildung, Assmann contends, was the Jews. Indeed, the Jews were "the last guardians of the original German idea of Bildung."[50] Yet this focus tends to blur the fact, emphasized in this volume, that upon entering the Bildungsbürgertum,[51] Jews laid claim not only to German Kultur and thus identity but also to the right to maintain their Jewish identity (as either a subsidiary or a parallel identity, be it conceived in ethnic, religious, and cultural

terms, or as a combination thereof).[52] Further, although
their cultural horizons may have been consistently liberal,
German Jews often sought to identify with German folk
culture (to wit, the novels of Berthold Auerbach [1812–
1882])[53] and cultivated a love of the German landscape that
was no less passionate than that of other Germans (to wit,
the German-Jewish youth movements, even those of a decidedly Zionist orientation),[54] not to speak of the German
Jews' attachment to the German language.[55]

Implicit in Mendelssohn's position as "the first German Jew" was his role as "the great *Vorbild* [model] of
the Jewish *Bildungsbürgertum* in Germany and beyond."[56]
But German society, even its most liberal representatives,
had difficulty in accepting him as a Jew and as a German
Aufklärer (follower of the Enlightenment, or *Aufklärung*).
It was not surprising, Rosenzweig later commented, that
Mendelssohn's contemporaries found him "incomprehensible" *(überbegreiflich)*. How were they "to grasp that there
stood before them not one person but two?"[57] Rosenzweig
faulted Mendelssohn for a lack of clarity regarding his twofold loyalty. Although Rosenzweig's critique, discussed at
length in Chapter 4, may be philosophically compelling,
it is rather unhistorical.[58] Even if Mendelssohn had been
more decisive in clarifying the basis of his dual identity as
a German (that is, by virtue of language and culture) and a
Jew (however defined), German society of his day was too
uncertain of its collective identity to entertain a pluralistic conception of its social and political fabric.

On the face of it, Mendelssohn's liberal opponents were
prompted by the intellectual and cultural monism of the
Enlightenment; they were beholden to reason as the arbi-
ter of one, indivisible, universal truth. Yet the votaries of
the Enlightenment did advocate tolerance of religious dis-
senters and those of differing opinions. The issue clearly

goes deeper. Mendelssohn was appealing for tolerance not
so much of Judaism's differing opinions—in fact, he sought
to show that intellectually the ancient faith of Israel was
in fundamental accord with the rational teachings of the
Enlightenment—as of Jewry's collective identity and religious culture.

That identity, Mendelssohn argued in *Jerusalem* (1783),
his famous defense of his allegedly contradictory fidelities,
is shaped by "historical truths"—which, while pointing to
God's manifest presence in his people's journey through
time, have decisively determined Israel's self-understanding—and by "the revealed ceremonial laws" that provide
the grammar of Jews' distinctive way of life.[59] Wilhelm
von Humboldt was quick to appreciate that behind Mendelssohn's impassioned defense of the rational structure of
Judaism was a healthy desire to preserve Jewish identity.
Although he was hardly persuaded by Mendelssohn's argument that Judaism was well suited to the project of the Enlightenment, Humboldt was nonetheless sympathetic to
the Jewish philosopher's abiding attachment to his ancestral way of life, which he understood as being dictated by a
desire to prevent the "national spirit" *(Nationalgeist)* of the
Jewish people from "perishing." This desire, he said, was
indeed "worthy of a thoughtful and perspicacious mind"
such as Mendelssohn's.[60]

But Humboldt was an exception. Most cultured Germans expected Mendelssohn and his fellow Jews to shed
their Judaism and primordial identity, if not forthwith, certainly incrementally and unfalteringly. This demand was
aggravated by the pervasive assumption that Judaism was
incompatible with liberal culture and sensibility.[61] The es-
teemed German liberal and patriot J. G. Fichte (1762–1814)
expressed this antagonism in a particularly truculent fashion when he suggested that the only way Jews would ever

truly be deserving of equal political rights would be "if one night we chop off their heads and replace them with new ones, in which there would not be one single Jewish idea."[62] This unabashedly malevolent remark was voiced by a respected philosopher in the preface to a work presenting his vision of a liberal, democratic Germany. More significantly, his animus toward the Jews was primed by his fear that even with their emancipation the Jews would remain a "state within a state," that they would not cease to preserve a distinct national identity and thus an allegiance superseding that required by German citizenship.[63]

To be sure, a venomous antisemitism informs Fichte's reflections, but it would be remiss not to note that there is a larger ideological issue at hand.[64] Clearly, as a German patriot—of a state that was yet to be—he was unable to conceive how one could have a "national culture and identity" aside from that of the envisioned German state. A Jewish national identity, or what today one is wont to call ethnic identity, implied to his mind allegiance to another, ergo alien, political entity. He simply did not contemplate the possibility that in the future German state one could be a German by citizenship and even culture and also affirm another cultural and even ethnic identity. In a word, Fichte's state—as well as that of most German liberals, not to speak of conservatives—was not pluralistic.[65]

One may perhaps speak of a tragic "mismeeting"[66] between Jews and Germans determined by differing "horizons of expectations."[67] Jews expected that the liberal discourse initiated by the Enlightenment would pave the way to a "neutral society"—a civil society in which one's religious and ethnic origins were irrelevant—supporting an open, democratic political state.[68] From Herder on, German liberals parted from that model of the modern state— dismissively associated in the minds of many Germans with France—as an elective or contractual association of individuals who have freely contracted to govern themselves according to democratic procedures and principles.[69] According to the model, nationality is not independent of citizenship—or, to express the notion philosophically, nationality does not have ontological priority in determining one's qualification for citizenship.

In deliberate opposition to the French model, the Germans developed an alternative conception of the state as principally serving a *Volksnation*, or a given people, which, ontologically prior to the state, is bound "less by an original accord than by a common relation [of its members] to some combination of historical memory, geography, kinship, tradition, mores, religion, and language."[70] These contrasting conceptions of the state are typological abstractions,[71] and there are important variations and overlappings between German and French political thought in the nineteenth and twentieth centuries, not to speak of the actual historical experience of both countries.[72]

With respect to the Jewish experience in Germany these models nonetheless have clear heuristic value, for they highlight what might be called the political anthropology of German-Jewish identity or, rather, identities.[73] From the perspective of these models, it would seem that the Jews of Germany constructed not only their political expectations but also their collective identity (certainly to the degree that it was grounded in those expectations) in a fundamentally different manner from that of the majority of Germans. Whereas the Jews adopted Bildung as the cultural and social matrix for the shaping of a modern identity, the Germans cultivated an identity as a Volksnation. The former was essentially ahistorical; the latter was grounded in such primordial factors as shared ethnic genealogy and historical memory. As Mosse incisively comments: "Jewish commitment to the humanistic ideal of Bildung was based on the correct perception that only through transcending a German past, which the Jews did not share, could Jews meet Germans on equal terms. Historical roots had played no part in Humboldt's concept of Bildung, and the classics upon whose knowledge the concept so largely depended were considered a universal heritage. Similarly, the concept of respectability was based upon a moral order and not dependent upon shared historical roots."[74] Led by the likes of Herder, Fichte, and the Grimm brothers, Germans constructed a historical memory and identity that ultimately reached back before the Enlightenment—the terminus a quo with which the Jews could and did identify—to Frederick Barbarossa (1121–1190), and the German tribes.[75]

It was precisely the perceived failure of the Jewish Bildungsbürgertum to identify with the primordial memories of Germany that irked the historian Heinrich von Treitschke. A liberal and ardent advocate of a united Germany, he lent his support and academic prestige to the antisemitic campaigns that swept Germany soon after the founding of the Second Reich. Declaring (with a now infamous slogan) that "the Jews are our misfortune,"[76] he justified the attacks on the Jews as "a brutal but natural reaction of German *national* feeling against a foreign element."[77] The Jews' "abrasive" conduct in business and culture (especially journalism), he argued, was ultimately to be attributed to their fundamental lack of what he called a "historical sense," manifest in their disregard of the sensibilities of the German nation. "For a nation which for centuries had ceased to possess a political history nothing seemed so alien as the historic sense. To the Jews, German veneration for the past appeared ludicrous, [in contrast to] modern France, which has broken with her history. They feel more at home in this new state [France], created, as it were, by pure reason."[78]

In elaborating this argument, Treitschke allowed himself a telling contradiction: The Jews' alleged loss of a historic sense—and their attendant failure to appreciate its importance for the Germans—corresponds to their abiding attachment to a Jewish *national* identity and its historical memories. In spite of the opportunity to assimilate and become part of the German nation, he charged, the Jews obstinately held fast to their national identity, their acquisition of German language and culture notwithstanding.[79] The political identity of the nascent German state was too delicate, he explained, to allow being Jewish to consist of more than a religious confession.[80] Membership in the German nation, he insisted, required full and unambiguous identification with the German Volk, with their historical memories and hopes.

One wonders whether Treitschke was not disingenuous in demanding that the Jews share in a German collective identity constructed as a Volksnation. What is clear, however, is that he denied the right of the Jews to regard themselves as both Jews and Germans, to maintain a Jewish national identity while claiming to be German. This was his clarion message in his debate with the historian Heinrich Graetz, author of an eleven-volume *History of the Jews* (1853–1882), who insisted that he was both a German patriot and a Jew proud of his Jewish "national" heritage and identity.[81] Treitschke fulminated, "On German soil there is no room for dual nationality [*Doppel-Nationalität*]."[82]

To be sure, Treitschke was not a racist and thus proclaimed his ready eagerness to embrace the assimilated Jew, the Jew who would link his or her destiny to that of the German nation and people.[83] He did not dispute the right of truly assimilated Jews to regard themselves as Germans, culturally and politically. Many German liberals shared this position, although they may secretly have questioned whether Jews, no matter how assimilated, could ever be inwardly bound to Germany. They perhaps would have endorsed the sentiments expressed by Wilhelm Raabe, who in his immensely popular novel *Der Hungerpastor* (1864) has a Jewish protagonist explain, "If any important issue is at stake, such as the fate, honor, or happiness of the German nation, we can descend into the arena and undergo suffering or death for the cause in question. On the contrary, our advantage consists precisely in the fact that we take part in such distress or death with an unbiased and Platonic animus. You [Aryans] struggle and suffer *pro demos*; we sacrifice ourselves for pure principle."[84]

The poet Stefan George, who profoundly appreciated the talent and devotion of the many Jews in his circle, expressed similar reservations. "The Jews make the best leaders," he conceded in 1911 to a friend of "pure" German provenance. "They are very gifted in the distribution and transformation of values. To be sure, they do not experience *(erleben)* things as elementally as we do. They are altogether different people. I will never allow them to become the majority in my Society or Year Book."[85] Apparently, he felt that Jews could never quite acquire that *Feingefühl* requisite to tap the philogenetic depths of the German soul.

Several months after Stefan George wrote his privately communicated reflections on the limitations of Jewish cultural integration, a debate erupted on the pages of the conservative literary journal *Der Kunstwart* exploring whether there are, indeed, cultural boundaries beyond which Jews are incapable of crossing or which they should at least not seek to transgress. Initiated by Jews, the "*Kunst-*

wart debate"—which figures prominently in this volume, especially Chapter 3—prompted some thoughtful Jews to reassess their twofold identity as Jews and Germans. The debate was not confined to the more than seventy statements submitted by Jews and non-Jews alike to the editors of *Der Kunstwart.* In Chapter 3 I discuss a correspondence between two young Jews, Walter Benjamin (1892–1940) and the poet Ludwig Strauss (1892–1953), on various issues raised in the debate. Their exchange anticipated a discourse that preoccupied German Jewry several years later.

The First World War was a watershed for German Jewry. The guns of August heralded an occasion for many Jews to demonstrate their patriotism and solidarity with fellow Germans. Heeding the Kaiser's spirited address at the outbreak of hostilities in which he declared that henceforth there were no longer any divisions among his subjects, only Germans, Jews with very few exceptions identified unequivocally with the cause of their beleaguered *Vaterland.*[86] Orthodox Jews no less than Reform Jews, Zionists, and the most assimilated Jews were confident that by fully sharing the sacrifices of war they would forge inviolable bonds of fraternity with other Germans.

Alas, it soon became apparent that their patriotism would hardly lift the barriers of suspicion and enmity that separated them from other Germans. In the midst of war and the ever mounting antisemitic sentiments coming from virtually all sectors of the German population,[87] the philosopher Hermann Cohen (1842–1918) recalled, undoubtedly with a pained sense of déjà vu, the words he had written close to fifty years earlier during the debate with Treitschke: "We younger people had indeed hoped that slowly we would be successfully integrated *(einzuleben)* by the 'nation of Kant' . . . , that we could in time let the love of the fatherland speak through us without restraint,

and that we would be allowed to cooperate with fully conscious pride in the tasks of the nation and with a sense
of equality. This trust has been broken; the old oppres-
sive anxiety has awakened again."[88] Though formally still
affirming the affinities between *Deutschtum und Judentum*—he used the phrase to entitle two wartime essays[89]—
Cohen subtly devised a new strategy for living with his
dual identity as a Jew and a German.

This turn in his thinking, examined in detail in Chapter 4, was first articulated in the aforementioned wartime
essays, in which he unapologetically asserts that Jews are
a "nationality"—a position that marked a radical departure from his previous insistence that Judaism had through
the grace of the German Enlightenment evolved into a
purely religious confession, charged with promoting "ethical monotheism." Within the German nation—a political
entity[90]—there are various nationalities, he said, Bavari-
ans, Prussians, Saxons, and so forth, with the Jews being
but one among them.[91] In the face of Germany's deepening xenophobia and antisemitism, Cohen defiantly spoke
of Germany as, in effect, a multinational or—if I be allowed to give his vision a contemporary twist—a multicultural state.[92]

Cohen's disciple Franz Rosenzweig (1886–1929) critically elaborated his mentor's affirmation of his twofold
identity as a German and a Jew. As is discussed in Chapter 4, Rosenzweig focused on the "and" linking the respective identities and traced the dialectical permutations
of this conjunction from Moses Mendelssohn's debut as
the first German Jew to his own generation of German
Jews, whose understanding of their defining cultural and
national identities was formed in the crucible of the
world war. Rosenzweig spoke of the shifting function of
the "and": it both separated and bridged the sides of the

equation. Mendelssohn's "and" was separative; in keep-
ing his Judaism and German cultural identity apart, he in
effect treated the latter as stronger and more compelling.
Throughout German-Jewish history, as the function of the
"and" shifts, the valence of either side of the equation
also changes, but without altering an essential asymmetry between the two; for the most part, German identity
is favored over Jewish affiliation. It is only with the maturing of the German Jew during the Jewish Renaissance
of the postwar years, according to Rosenzweig, that the
"and" came to signify a healthy balance between covalent
spiritual estates.

Rosenzweig's spiritual journey became emblematic of
the Jewish Renaissance.[93] From the midst of radical assimilation, which had brought him to the threshold of conversion to Christianity, he became a deeply pious Jew, affirming Judaism as a vital intellectual and religious reality.[94]
For him as for others, the Jewish Renaissance was as much
an expression of a newfound resolve to assert one's Jewish identity as it was a movement of cultural and religious renewal. This self-assertion was undoubtedly most
defiantly and unapologetically expressed in the name of
a journal that Martin Buber (1878–1965) founded in 1916,
Der Jude (The Jew).[95] Clearly, this organ, which immediately became one of the finest literary and cultural reviews
of its day, marked a new chapter in German-Jewish self-
understanding and, I must add, self-representation. Jewishness no longer pointed merely to one's ancestral origins or
confessional affiliation but was (as variously defined) now
regarded as an engaging source of personal and collective
significance. Few would say, however, that their newly
affirmed Judaism at all diminished their attachment to
German culture and identity. Most would surely endorse
Rosenzweig's words to a friend: "I believe my return to

Judaism *(Verjudung)* has not made me a worse but a better German. I do not in any way whatsoever view the generation [of Jews] before us as better Germans."[96]

What distinguished his generation from the previous one, Rosenzweig claimed, was the "and" joining their identities as Jews and Germans. For him and those who shared in the Jewish Renaissance, the "and" conjoined equally commanding identities, whereas formerly Jews had been uncertain how to coordinate their competing affiliations and, given the struggle to attain Bildung and political emancipation, naturally tended to give greater attention to acquiring a German cultural and national identity. Confident that his generation had found the resources to sustain their covalent identity as Germans and Jews, Rosenzweig spoke of Germany as a New Babylon.

The vision of a New Babylon may be seen as a revision of Heinrich Heine's prophecy of a New Jerusalem arising from the meeting of Germans and Jews, the product of an "elective affinity" *(Wahlverwandtschaft)*. These two "ethical nations" *(Völker der Sittlichkeit)*, the poet mused, were destined to "merge," creating a New Jerusalem on the banks of the Rhine, "the home of the sacred word, the mother soil of prophecy, and the citadel of pure spirituality."[97] In contrast, Rosenzweig's New Babylon did not bespeak a merger or a graced sublation of the German and Jewish spirit. Rather, Rosenzweig envisioned Germany as a "land of two rivers" *(Zweistromland)*, giving it the literal name of biblical Babylonia (Naharayim), which stood at the confluence of the Euphrates and the Tigris. In Babylonia, nurtured by the waters of two great rivers, Judaism flourished and reached the height of its spiritual creativity, the crowning achievement being the Babylonian Talmud, a multivolume compendium of religious law, ethical and homiletic teachings, and wisdom. In Germany,

Rosenzweig affirmed, the modern Jew also stands by two nurturing sources, German humanistic culture and a Judaism challenged and revalorized by the modern experience. Rosenzweig voiced the hope that what would emerge from this meeting—preeminently a dialogue *within* the soul of the German Jew—would, indeed, be a New Babylon. Alas, the possibilities of realizing a New Babylon on German soil were brutally aborted by the rise of Hitler and his Satanic forces—hence the title of the concluding chapter of this volume, "Franz Rosenzweig's Eulogy for German Jewry." "Eulogy" thus refers to Rosenzweig's critical but hopeful reading of the spiritual biography of German Jewry, which by dint of his vision also serves as a mournful homage to a community destroyed before it could reach the fullness of its promise.

The eulogy is written in the voice of Rosenzweig, who, dying in 1929, predeceased his community. His "words" could address the life and promise of German Jewry but not assess its legacy for those who bereave its death. An epilogue to Rosenzweig's eulogy is thus called for—my understanding of the legacy of German Jewry based on the perspective adumbrated in this volume.

Chapter Two

History and *Kultur*
The German-Jewish Perspective

In June 1853 the renowned German botanist Wilhelm Hofmeister had occasion to visit the home of a Jewish colleague, Nathaniel Pringsheim, who lived in an elegant Berlin residence. After what was manifestly a delightful evening, Hofmeister wrote to his wife in Leipzig, bemusedly noting that the Pringsheim home was "filled with ladies—[innumerable] sisters and an elderly mother."[1] Hofmeister was clearly enthralled by these ladies, by their culture and convivial, urbane conversation. These "Berlin Jewesses," as Hofmeister admiringly called them, were the aunts of Thomas Mann's wife, Katja.[2] Thomas had met Katja at the University of Munich, at which she was the first German woman to study.[3] Indeed, Katja was the first of her sex in Bavaria to take—and pass—the matriculation exams required for university study. Katja prepared for the exams—the so-called *Abitur*—with the aid of special tutors, for it was not until the early twentieth century that German-born women were allowed to attend full-fledged gymnasia in Germany, not to speak of attending the universities.[4]

Since the time of Moses Mendelssohn's daughter Dorothea (1764–1839) and her famed literary salon, Jewish women were prominently associated with German Kultur, or high culture.[5] In Berlin, as elsewhere in Central Europe, the salons conducted by Jewish women were a significant feature of the intellectual landscape of cultural life, especially in the latter decades of the eighteenth century and the early decades of the next. Everybody who was anybody —Fichte, Heine, Wilhelm von Humboldt, Schleiermacher, the Schlegel brothers—eagerly sought an invitation to one of these salons, especially the one hosted by the irascible but brilliant Rahel Levine Varnhagen (1771–1833). Until the twentieth century women were largely excluded from the formal institutions of Kultur, a fact that renders the cultural attainments of Jewish women that much more impressive.

To be sure, special sociohistorical circumstances prompted Jewish women to rush to the waters of Kultur, and they did so with the first breach of the walls of the ghetto. Their devotion to the most refined expressions of German culture—art, literature, and music—was, however, at bottom indicative of German Jewry's uniquely passionate embrace of the ethic of Bildung, the humanistic ideal, born of the German Enlightenment, of self-cultivation of one's intellectual and moral faculties through a study of literature and philosophy, and the refinement of one's aesthetic sensibilities through the arts and music.[6] Unlike the word "education," the lexical equivalent in English, *Bildung*, as Herder stressed, denotes a continuous, never-ending process: a ceaseless quest for the good, the true, and the beautiful. For the votaries of Bildung, aesthetic sensibility and grace—which represented disciplined passion and a harmony of form—became emblematic of their cultural ideal. Indeed, the beautiful "symbolized the ideal of a shared humanity," for it is a quality of the spirit, as Humboldt, Goethe, and Schiller taught, that all individuals can attain, regardless of the accidents of birth, nationality, and religion.[7] Bildung was, accordingly, regarded as "the knighthood of modernity,"[8] which, unlike its medieval antecedent, was opened to Jews and non-Jews alike. No wonder Jews embraced the ideal of Bildung with such eagerness and devotion.

Jews were quick to realize that Bildung and Kultur were the gateways to bourgeois respectability, if not acceptance.[9] Although social acceptance may have proved elusive, respectability seemed attainable, for it was in large measure self-referential, or, as a cultured German would put it, respectability does not require a dependent genitive. Bildung thus by its very nature conferred respectability on the erstwhile residents of the ghetto, at least in their own eyes. Ever since Mendelssohn, the son of the Torah scribe Mendel of Dessau, gained acclaim as a *Kulturmensch* and was hailed by his fellow Aufklärer of the eighteenth century as the German Socrates, Bildung—and the quest for the true, the good, and the beautiful—became an integral part of the German-Jewish identity and self-image.

Yet, "with the passage of time," as George Mosse noted, "*Bildung* became detached from the individual and his struggle for self-cultivation and was transformed into a kind of religion."[10] And it was as a kind of religion that Bildung and Kultur became venerated by all strata of German Jewry. German Jews made—if I may be permitted a pun—a cult of Kultur. In homage to the pantheon of German culture, they often called their male offspring Gotthold Ephraim after the beloved Lessing, and many adopted Schiller as a family name.[11] Although I know of no Jews who consciously called their children after Goethe, the poet was honored in virtually every Jewish household. It is said only somewhat hyperbolically that a set of his writings graced every Jewish home and was the standard bar mitzvah and confirmation present.[12] Many a rabbi wove citations from Goethe into his sermons. In the years im-

mediately following the First World War, the Jews of Frankfurt am Main, Goethe's city of birth, were especially proud
of Rabbi Anton Nehamia Nobel, who displayed an un-
paralleled mastery of Goethe in his legendary sermons.[13]
The fact that Nobel, an Orthodox rabbi, was also regarded
as one of the leading Talmudic authorities in Germany
only enhanced his reputation among the Jews as a *Goethe-
kenner*.

Already in Goethe's lifetime, Jews seemed to display an
especial affection for him. Goethe's intimate friend Friedrich Wilhelm Riemer observed that "the educated among
[the Jews] were on the whole more obliging and steady
in the adoration of [Goethe's] person as well as his writings than many of his own coreligionists. They do reveal
in general more pleasing attention and flattering participation than a national German, and their quick power of
comprehension, their penetrating intellect, their peculiar
wit render them a more sensitive audience than what re-
grettably can be found among the often somewhat dull and
slow-to-comprehend genuine Germans."[14] Note Riemer's
adjective "genuine"—in the German it has a special inflec-
tion, *Echt- und Ur-Deutschen*.[15] Parenthetically, Riemer
also reports that "[Jewish] women possess those talents [of
intellect and comprehension] at times in even more ami-
able form." Thus, Riemer continued, "it happened that
Goethe was willing to present his recent poetical produc-
tions to them [Jewish women] either individually or in
groups . . . , for he could always be assured of a certain response."[16]

On the eve of the First World War, writing to the poet
Ludwig Strauss, who was to become Martin Buber's son-
in-law, the youthful Walter Benjamin contended that Jewish intellectuals—the *Literatenjuden*—were ordained to
preserve the critical mind and the ethic of Bildung; in-

deed, he averred, this task had become the very essence of Jewishness. To appreciate fully what is entailed by this Jewishness, Benjamin urged his correspondent to consult Goethe. It is only through the study of Goethe, Benjamin explained, that the nature of Jewishness is fully revealed.[17]

Kant was perhaps even more honored by German Jewry. In the midst of the First World War, the philosopher Hermann Cohen sought to remind his embattled fatherland of its cultural pedigree and obligations. With patriotic pathos he declared: "Every German must know his Schiller and his Goethe and carry them in his heart with the intimacy of love. Yet this intimacy presupposes that he has won a rudimentary understanding also of Kant."[18] Cohen insisted that Kant is and must remain the bedrock of German humanism and Kultur. Hence, in a defiant speech before the Kant Gesellschaft of Berlin, he castigated those who would allow the euphoria of war to elevate German warriors and statesmen above German poets and thinkers. Germany—Cohen proclaimed—"is and remains in continuity with the eighteenth century and its cosmopolitan humanity."[19]

Cohen, who died in 1918, several years after his retirement from the University of Marburg, devoted his life to fostering the legacy of Kant. He was, furthermore, convinced that Kant's ethical idealism not only gave pristine expression to the German soul but also bore a fundamental affinity to the ethical monotheism of the Hebrew Bible and of the rabbis. Cohen's teachings were eagerly endorsed by German Jewry, and his famous essays on the affinity between Judaism and Kant seem to have made their way into every Jewish home, certainly every rabbi's study.

The depth of the German Jew's allegiance to Kant is charmingly expressed in a volume published in the 1920s by one Salomo (Solomon) Friedländer entitled *Kant für*

Kinder. Written in the form of a catechism, the volume was meant to introduce children to the ethical teachings of Kant. In typical German fashion, Friedländer posed the question "Wer ist auf diesem Wege [zur Wahrheit] unser treuster Führer?" (Who is our truest guide—*Führer*—on the way to truth?) The youthful readers of this catechism are instructed to reply: "Immanuel Kant!"[20]

A special affection was reserved for the revered Gotthold Ephraim Lessing (1729–1781), Mendelssohn's faithful friend and consistent proponent of Jewish dignity and civil rights. When, in the early 1880s, funds were to be raised to commission a monument in honor of Lessing, Jews appropriately led the subscription.[21] And in 1929, the two hundredth anniversary of Lessing's birth, the Jewish community of Germany was virtually alone in marking the occasion.[22]

German Jewry not only pursued culture as a nigh religious value but also, when permitted, entered the venerated citadels of culture and Bildung: the universities. They did so in numbers so disproportionate to their representation in the population of Germany and elsewhere in Central Europe, and with such success, that Albert Einstein is said to have remarked that it was as though the Israelites had spent the past two millennia of the Exile preparing for their entrance examinations.[23] The rush of Jews to the universities of Central Europe gave birth to another quip: "Doktor ist ein jüdischer Vorname."[24]

The energetic entrance of the Jews into the Bildungsbürgertum—the educated bourgeoisie—of Central Europe led to a spectacular flowering of Jewish creativity. Under the aegis of German Kultur, Jews contributed to all spheres of modern culture. Children and grandchildren of rabbinic scholars and impoverished peddlers alike found themselves at the forefront of European science and letters.

But cruel misfortune overtook German Jewry: less than one hundred and fifty years after the death of Moses Mendelssohn, who inaugurated Jewry's covenant with German culture, demonic forces ripped that covenant to pieces. The flower that once was German Jewry was torn at its roots and trampled under foot with a Manichaean fury. Since the Holocaust, sentiment and inconsolable grief have led many to eulogize and unwittingly mystify the cultural achievements of German Jewry. Celebrating the Jewish intellectuals of Germany and Central Europe, George Steiner speaks of them as "meta-rabbis" and notes that "the Jewish element had been largely dominant in the revolutions of thought and of sensibility experienced by Western man over these last one hundred and twenty years. . . . Without Marx, Freud, or Kafka, without Schoenberg or Wittgenstein, the spirit of modernity, the reflexes of argument and uncertainty whereby we conduct our inner lives, would not be conceivable."[25] The treatment of the Jewish intellectuals of modern Germany and Central Europe as the prophets of modernity—or as one scholar has it, "prophets without honor"[26]—is animated by an understandable affection and nostalgia; but, I fear, it is hardly illuminating.[27] This approach, shared by many, apodictically assumes that "Jewish genius" was unique—and somehow glosses over the Kants, the Hegels, the Nietzsches, the Jungs, the Thomas Manns, the Beethovens, the Bruckners. The celebration of German Jewry's intellectual preeminence tacitly, and sometimes not so tacitly, also appeals to the allegedly superior intelligence of the Jews.[28] On purely methodological grounds, one is obliged to endorse Peter Gay's demand, made in a fit of exasperation: "There is a historical and sociological study that desperately needs to be undertaken: that of stupid Jews."[29]

The assumption of a fast correlation of intelligence and

intellectual and artistic creativity violates what we know
about the complex cognitive and sociological nature of
intellectual attainment and creativity. Casting the question of the intellectual preeminence of German Jewry in
the light of the disproportionate number of Jews in virtually every facet of Central European cultural life can
also be misleading. True, in Germany the Jews never constituted much more than 1 percent of the total population; and the proportion declined steadily as the citizenry
grew between 1871 and 1933 from 41 million to some 65
million while the number of Jews—oscillating between
500,000 and 600,000—hardly increased. The demographic
proportions were similar in other countries of the German *Kulturbereich,* the regions of Europe under the sway
of the German language and culture. But it is crucial to
note that the Jews tended to concentrate in the major
cities, the central arenas of modern culture. With their
embourgeoisement, they were drawn to the urban centers
in numbers far exceeding those of the general population.
Thus, whereas in the nineteenth century the total population of Berlin increased twelvefold, the Jewish population of the city increased twenty-sevenfold, constituting
5 percent of the total population of the Prussian capital.[30]
In the nineteenth century, Budapest—which maintained
a bilingual cultural life, Hungarian and German—was the
fastest-growing city in Europe. In 1789 there were only 114
Jews in the Hungarian capital; by 1920 there were well
over 200,000, constituting close to 25 percent of the population.[31] The Jewish profile of the city was so prominent
that it was jocularly called "Judapest."[32] The same pattern holds true for other major cities of Germany and the
Austro-Hungarian Empire.[33]

Breaking down the figures according to occupational
distribution shows how pronounced the embourgeoise-

ment of Central European Jewry was.[34] To illustrate this, some statistics detailing the Jews' dramatic, overawing entrance into the secular educational system will suffice. "By 1860 the percentage of Jewish [male] children attending secondary schools [in Prussia] was three, even four times as high as that of children of other confessions. In the following decades the percentage was even higher."[35] The numbers for those attending universities are even more astounding: During the last decade of the nineteenth century, "for every 100,000 males of each [religious] denomination in Prussia, there studied in Prussian universities 33 Catholics, 58 Protestants and 519 Jews."[36] At the German university of Prague, in the years that Franz Kafka was there, close to 50 percent of the student body was Jewish.[37] In 1890 Jews composed 33.6 percent of the students at the University of Vienna; the percentage of Jews studying at the medical faculty was even higher.[38] And if I may return to Jewish women for a moment: In Prussia in 1901, when women were finally permitted to take the Abitur examinations, which qualify those who pass for university study, the first contingent of fifty-six women included seventeen Jews, or 30 percent of the total.[39] It has been estimated that in 1901 in all of Germany the percentage of Jewish women enrolled in gymnasia was 42, compared to only 4 percent of gentile women.[40]

The Jews' rapid and remarkably successful passage into the burgeoning urban middle class provided the social and economic basis for the Jews' entrance into the Bildungsbürgertum [41] and, accordingly, renders their disproportionate participation in the high culture of Germany and Central Europe far less mystifying. Their embourgeoisement, however, does not fully explain the enthusiasm with which they adopted the culture of Bildung. Nor, for that matter, does it adequately illuminate why economically less fortu-

nate Jews honored Bildung and Kultur. Here we must look
to the historic conjunction in eighteenth-century Germany of the Enlightenment — die Aufklärung — and the initial struggle for Jewish emancipation. The advocates of the
Enlightenment, such as Lessing, were often in the forefront
of efforts to extend tolerance to the Jews and improve their
status. Thus the Jews of Germany naturally viewed the Aufklärer as their allies and the Aufklärung as the culture and
ethos that would sponsor a life of dignity and opportunity
beyond the degradation and confinement of the ghetto.
Specifically, the Jews were inspired by the promise that
Bildung and a culture guided by intellect would sponsor
their citizenship in the new era — a tolerant and humane
era — envisioned by the Enlightenment thinkers.

The alignment of Jewish hopes and passions with
the humanistic ideals of the German Enlightenment pro-
ceeded with such facility and brought such an efflores-
cence of Jewish intellect and talent that German Jews often
spoke of a unique inner relation between Deutschtum and
Judentum, of a propitious affinity between German and
Jewish intellectual and cultural values. To be sure, there
was no small measure of apologetic fantasy informing
these observations. It is nonetheless intriguing to consider
the cultural correspondences between Judaism and German humanistic culture. Permit me to indicate, however
adumbratively, what appear to be three structural affinities between the two traditions. Classical Judaism and
German Bildung both have a concept of high culture that
attributes an intrinsic, overarching value to education —
grounded in canonical texts — and learning; both have a
concept of knowledge as anti-eudaemonistic and hence
affirm knowledge as preeminently serving truth and not
principally the promotion of earthly happiness or some
instrumental aim; and both uphold an ethical idealism,

namely, the conviction that education and the quest for knowledge are properly dedicated to the illumination of what one "ought" to do in the service of the true and the good. These affinities perhaps explain the depth of Jewish attachment to German culture, an attachment that, incidentally, extended beyond Germany and the German Kulturbereich. German thought and letters engaged the imagination of the Jewish intelligentsia of tsarist Russia and the Balkan countries and often England and the Americas.

The Jewish experience of German Kultur was not unambiguous, however. As R. J. Zwi Werblowsky has incisively put it, "European Jewry did not enter modern society in a long process of 'endogenous' gestation and growth, but they plunged into it as the walls of the ghetto were being breached, with a bang, though not without prolonged whimpers."[42] This was especially true of the Jewries of Germany and Central Europe. In hastening to identify with German Kultur, the Jews often viewed their own culture — despite its structural similarities with German humanism — as an impediment, as ill suited to the cognitive and axiological requirements of the modern world. The tradition and folkways of their ancestral faith were not infrequently regarded as unmodern, even embarrassingly anachronistic. Jews often internalized the negative image of Judaism that prevailed even in enlightened circles. In the extreme, the attendant loss of Jewish self-esteem led to that insidious disease known as Jewish self-hatred.[43] Most often, acculturated German Jews were simply bewildered; perhaps despite themselves they were still bound to their primordial culture and identity while having yet to find a firm footing in German culture and society. Kafka pinpointed the tragedy of the cultured Jew when he observed that "most . . . wanted to leave Jewishness behind them, and

their fathers approved of this, but vaguely (this vagueness
was what was outrageous to them). But with their hind legs
they were still glued to their father's Jewishness and with
their waving front legs they found no new ground."[44]

The sources of this psychic imbalance may be found,
paradoxically, in Lessing's great tribute to the Jews, his
play of 1779, *Nathan the Wise.* The hero of this parable
of tolerance is a Jew, Nathan, a manifestly kind and wise
man. Patently modeled on Moses Mendelssohn, Nathan
is Lessing's spokesperson for the virtues of the Enlightenment: tolerance and unbiased, rational judgment:

> Nathan is above all good.
> How free from prejudice
>   his lofty soul,
> His heart to every virtue
>   how unlocked,
> With every lovely feeling
>   how familiar.[45]

Not surprisingly, German Jewry regarded *Nathan the
Wise* as its spiritual Magna Carta.[46] From the Jewish point
of view there was nonetheless something profoundly troubling about the play, at least regarding the portrayal of
Nathan. Most Jews revered Lessing too much and prized
the play too much to dare to raise any questions. Perhaps
unfortuitously, it was a great non-Jewish historian and philosopher, Wilhelm Dilthey (1833–1911), who was to offer
one of the most incisive analyses of the tragic flaw of the
play. The value of Nathan's personality, Dilthey noted, is
independent of the historical religion to which he formally
belonged.[47] Nathan's many engaging virtues have nothing
to do with his Jewishness, as if it were of no consequence
to the shaping of his soul. This was Lessing's intended mes-

sage. He clearly wished that his audience would draw the conclusion that religious differences were utterly irrelevant to an individual's humanity and capacity to achieve culture and moral virtue. This is undoubtedly the most enduring—and, one would hope, indisputable—teaching of the Enlightenment. The rub, however, as Rosenzweig observed, is that there are "no children" at the end of Lessing's play [48]—certainly no Jewish children nor Muslim children, nor, for that matter, Christian children.

In seeking a neutral ground beyond differences of religion and nationality, the Enlightenment thinkers in effect sought to neutralize the significance of personal background. [49] Through the sapient and tender Nathan, Lessing called upon his fellow Germans to relegate those differences to the province of sentiment and personal taste, leaving one's humanity to come to the fore unfettered by the ultimately unimportant issue of one's religious and ethnic provenance. Neither Dilthey nor Rosenzweig challenged Lessing's premise that we are all human beings despite our differences; but they also argued that those differences may in fact nurture our humanity, that our humanity may also be expressed in and through our different religious communities and distinctive cultures. The Enlightenment's concept of tolerance, then, had its flip side. As Rosenzweig expressed it in a letter to Martin Buber: "The Christian ignored the Jew in order to tolerate him; and the Jew ignored the Christian in order to facilitate that tolerance." [50]

Implicit here is a critique not only of the Enlightenment's conception of a neutral "high" culture but also of the presupposition that such a culture is a higher culture. Mendelssohn already recognized this as the conviction underlying the Enlightenment's conception of Kultur when he objected to Lessing's view of history as an edu-

cative process in which humankind, by traversing various
levels of culture, attains intellectual and moral maturity.[51]
In a rare rebuke of his friend and mentor, Mendelssohn
declared: "I, for my part, cannot conceive of the education of the human race as my late friend Lessing imagined
it under the influence of I-don't-know-which historian of
mankind. One pictures the collective entity of the human
race as an individual person and believes that Providence
sent it to school here on earth, in order to raise it from
childhood to manhood. In reality, the human race is — if the
metaphor is appropriate — in almost every century, child,
adult, and old man at the same time, though in different
places and regions of the world."[52] Though acknowledging
progress in the arts, sciences, and philosophy, Mendelssohn refused to ascribe any moral value to such progress:
"As far as the human race as a whole is concerned, you
will find no steady development that brings it closer to
perfection. Rather do we see the human race in its totality
slightly oscillate; it never took a few steps forward without soon afterwards, and with redoubled speed, sliding
back to its previous position. . . . Individual man advances,
but mankind continually fluctuates within fixed limits,
while maintaining, on the whole, about the same degree
of morality, in all periods — the same amount of religion
and irreligion, of virtue and vice, of felicity and misery."[53]

To Mendelssohn's mind Lessing's conception of the Enlightenment as the culmination of humankind's historical
progress was a dubious doctrine, for he discerned in it a per-
nicious tendency to differentiate peoples and their respective cultures and religions according to a scale of historical-
cum-moral development.[54] Such a doctrine, Mendelssohn
protested, tore at the very heart of the Enlightenment,
namely, the principle of natural law, according to which
the eternal truths of nature — the eternal verities of reli-

gion and morality—are accessible to all human beings at all times and places. Only the principle of natural law, Mendelssohn affirmed, can further the Enlightenment and promote a shared humanity [55]—a proposition, incidentally, well appreciated by the architects of the American constitution.[56]

The doctrine of historical progress not only threatened to eclipse the principle of natural law that in Mendelssohn's judgment sustained the Enlightenment but also sponsored a cosmopolitanism that for Jews was at once alluring and unsettling. As the historical culmination of all human experience, the Enlightenment was theoretically open to all cultures. All cultures fed into the evolving Kultur of the educated German and European.[57] In this sense, Kultur was a syncretistic summary—or *Aufhebung*, as Hegel would put it—of all previous cultures.

Educated Germans regarded themselves as custodians of world culture, privileged curators of the cumulative wisdom of distant and not so distant cultures. The treasures —material and spiritual—of these cultures graced their libraries and imagination. Refracted through the learned perspective of German Kultur—that is, through the consciousness of thinking, reflective humankind—these cultures gained a refinement and depth that they presumably lacked when isolated in the place and time of their emergence. A Sumerian Temple placed in the Pergamon Museum of Berlin was said to acquire a dignity and a cultural significance far surpassing its original impact or intent.[58]

This syncretistic pluralism exercised a spell on Jews, as is attested by an exhibit of Freud's splendid collection of antiquities mounted in 1990.[59] It also meant for many Jews that Judaism could be acknowledged as one of the eclectic cultures composing German Kultur. What this often im-

plied is related through the tale of the founders of modern
Jewish studies, the so-called *Wissenschaft des Judentums.*
The inspiration of a group of Jewish students at the University of Berlin in 1819, Wissenschaft des Judentums was initially intended to counter the contention—propounded by
Lessing and especially by Hegel—that the Jewish contribution to world culture was exhausted with the Hebrew Bible.
Through rigorous scholarship *(Wissenschaft)*, the youthful proponents of this new discipline held that postbiblical
Judaism irrefutably contributed in innumerable and decisive ways to the shaping of world culture, particularly as it
unfolded in Europe. But in assigning Judaism a more hon-
orable place in the cultural history of Europe than Lessing
and Hegel did, the founders of Wissenschaft des Judentums
also conceded that with the dawn of Kultur, of a genuinely
cosmopolitan culture, it was no longer necessary or proper
for Judaism to continue as a distinctive culture. Moritz
Steinschneider (1816–1907), one of the founding figures of
modern Jewish studies, unabashedly explained that he and
his colleagues sought to provide Judaism with a "decent
burial," with its deeds judiciously assessed and eulogized.[60]

With the emergence of Europe, as the cosmopolitan
ideal was then called, Judaism must be prepared to dis-
solve into the larger whole—this was the demand of history, proclaimed Eduard Gans (1798–1839), a devoted student of Hegel's and president of the society that promoted
the founding of Wissenschaft des Judentums: "This, then,
is the demand of present-day Europe: the Jews must completely incorporate themselves into [the social and cultural
fabric of Europe]. This demand, the logical consequence of
the European principle, must be put to the Jews. Europe
would be untrue to itself and to its essential nature if it
did not put forth this demand. Now the time for this demand, and its fulfillment, has come."[61] Gans consoled his

fellow Jews in typical Hegelian fashion: "To merge is not to perish *(aufgehen ist nicht untergehen)*; as a stream lives on in the ocean into which it flows," so Judaism will be preserved in the memory and heartbeat of Europe.[62] It is the task of Jewish studies as an academic discipline to ensure that this memory remains alive and that Europe—and Germany—remains cognizant of its debt to Judaism.

Some Jews heeded Gans's call for a dialectic hara-kiri,[63] but many more remained confused as to the place of Judaism in German high culture. In spite of the ambiguities, they remained true to the Enlightenment ideal of Bildung and Kultur, even when German thought and culture developed in other, more romantic, less cosmopolitan directions. The very Bildung that promised to integrate the Jews into the common fabric of humanity left them in the end virtually isolated within a German society overtaken by nationalism and its invidious myths and symbols.[64] As German romantics and chauvinists sought to promote a Teutonic culture divorced from the Enlightenment, Jews tended to hold firm to the vision of a shared humanity guarded by the supremacy of reason and Kultur. Surely, as a beleaguered minority, the Jews of Germany had an interest in emphasizing what united rather than that which divided people. Their defiant loyalty to the Enlightenment, however, took on heroic proportions when, in October 1933, the Jüdische Kulturbund—established by the Nazis to reghettoize Jewish cultural life—chose to inaugurate its theatrical program with none other than Lessing's *Nathan the Wise*.[65]

Tellingly, the directors of the Kulturbund performance of Lessing's play introduced a slight but significant change in the plot that subtly dramatized the plight of German Jewry in that tragic hour. Lessing had concluded the play with Nathan's joyful witnessing of the Christian's and the Muslim's acknowledgment of each other as brothers and their departure arm in arm; thereupon, Nathan, "aglow with gratification, exits." In the 1933 production, "Nathan stayed behind, proud and lonely at the front of the stage, as the curtain fell."[66] Though alone, Nathan stood erect, as if to remind his tormentors of an alternative German tradition—a tradition of tolerance affirming the humanity binding Jew and non-Jew. There alone on the stage, Nathan also tacitly declared that in spite of all efforts to cut him off from the family of humanity, he resolutely refused to be ghettoized in spirit.[67]

With Hitler's accession to power, German Jewry mounted a "spiritual resistance" to Nazi tyranny,[68] finding no more effective way to do so than by affirming German Kultur, even in the death camps. They also set out in those dark years to redefine their relation to Judaism and its place within the larger compass of Kultur. In the shadow of the Holocaust these questions had a certain poignancy, although they had long been the obsessive preoccupation of German Jewry. "From Mendelssohn on," as Rosenzweig once noted, "our entire people has subjected itself to the torture of this embarrassing questioning; the entire Jewish-ness of every individual has squirmed on the needle point of this 'why.'"[69] The hold of Judaism on the Jew was no longer self-evident. Frequently, the question was posed as, Deutschtum and Judentum—German culture and Judaism —can the twain meet?

The boundlessly prolific cultural critic and anarchist Gustav Landauer (1870–1919) framed the question from the perspective of the humanistic conception of German Kul-tur. If through the agency of Deutschtum the Jew had become a citizen of the world, how was he or she to live with multiple cultural filiations? Landauer's reply—the epi-graph to this volume—was a proud affirmation of cosmo-politanism, or what we now call cultural pluralism: "I have never had the need to simplify myself or to create an artificial unity through denial; I accept my complexity and hope to be even more many-sided than I am now aware of."[70] Landauer did not deny the Jewish element in his cultural and spiritual universe; it was just one of many, the multiplication of which he joyful anticipated.

Landauer's friend Martin Buber concurred despite his Zionist sympathies. Noting that the modern Jew does indeed dwell in multiple cultures, Buber held that it would be chimerical, if not inane, to try and "expel, relinquish or overcome the one or the other; it would be senseless . . . to try to shed the culture of the world about us, a culture that, in the final analysis, has been assimilated by [our] innermost forces . . . and has become an integral part of ourselves. We [Jews] need to be conscious of the fact that we are a cultural admixture, in a more poignant sense than any other people."[71] Buber hastened to add: "We do not, however, wish to be slaves to this admixture, but its masters."[72]

Mastery of the admixture is assured only if one is sovereign—if one is equally at home—in each of the cultures to which one lays claim. Such sovereignty, moreover, assures that each constituent culture of one's pluralistic identity retains its integrity and distinctive intellectual and spiritual passion. Specifically, Buber maintained, to be genuinely both a Jew and a German, one must take both these cultural identities seriously, attending to each with affection and an informed commitment.

It is the sublime and primal destiny of the Jewish people, Rosenzweig taught, to embody—and master—an ensemble of cultures. He pointed out that Abraham, the father of the Hebrew nation, was born in Mesopotamia —Naharayim, a "land of two rivers." The Jews, remaining true to their origins in Naharayim—which, as already noted, Rosenzweig rendered in his and Buber's German

translation of the Hebrew scriptures as *Zweistromland*—
are sustained by a confluence of sources, an ever replenish-
ing inflow of diverse cultural streams. Thus, Rosenzweig
gave a volume of his writings on both general and Jewish
themes—which he deliberately did not separate—the title
Zweistromland.[73] The Jew resides on the banks of two cultures, that of the world and that of Judaism. This dual allegiance is the ground of an authentic pluralism, a pluralism
that preserves the Jew's integrity as both a Jew and a citizen of the world.

Let me conclude this chapter with a story, a true story
that is somehow also a parable or, perhaps better, a mid-
rash: It is said of Rabbi Leo Baeck (1873–1956), the noble
shepherd of German Jewry during its last tragic hours, that
he introduced a small but ever so momentous change in
his morning routine. It was his wont each morning after
prayers to read a page from the Talmud, then a passage from
a Greek play in the original Greek. As the dark clouds of
the Third Reich gathered, he changed his routine. He now
read from the Hebrew prophets and then from the German
classics—Kant, Goethe, and Schiller.[74]

Chapter Three

The German-Jewish Parnassus

"Two souls, alas, dwell in my breast."
GOETHE, *Faust*

In a now famous essay of 1919, the American social philosopher Thorstein Veblen spoke of the "intellectual preeminence of Jews in modern Europe," apodictically pointing to the fact that individuals of Jewish origin "count for more than their proportionate share in the intellectual life of western civilization."[1] With manifest admiration, even affection, he celebrated "the intellectually gifted Jew[s]" of Europe who find themselves in "the vanguard of modern inquiry."[2] But, as Gershom Scholem observed some fifty years later, "it was precisely [their] 'preeminence' that was to spell the doom of the Jews of Germany."[3]

Accepting the gracious invitation of the Aufklärung to participate in the shaping of modern culture, the Jews of Germany eagerly acquired the requisite education and enthusiastically assumed a role in German intellectual and artistic life. Their spirited devotion to modern culture awed all but also engendered a certain uneasiness from the very beginning. I am reminded of the philosopher Eduard Gans—said to be perhaps Hegel's favorite student—who, barred from an academic appointment because of his religious affiliation, lamented: "I belong to that unfortunate class of human beings which is hated because it is uneducated, and persecuted because it tries to educate itself."[4] The resentment of Jews of cultural and intellectual attainment became increasingly palpable, even in liberal circles. As self-conscious heirs to the Enlightenment, however, liberals by and large felt it was improper to broach in public their misgivings regarding the role that emancipated Jewry had assumed in Germany's cultural life. Jews wedded to the liberal ethos certainly preferred to ignore the issue.[5] The silence was unceremoniously broken in March 1912 with a brash article, "The German-Jewish Parnassus," published in the prestigious cultural review *Der Kunstwart.*[6]

Written by a young Jewish scholar of German literature, Moritz Goldstein (1880–1972), the article provoked a debate that reverberated for several years through the German press.[7] Goldstein obviously touched a raw nerve when he asserted: "We Jews are administrating the spiritual property of a nation which denies our right and our ability to do so."[8] He explained: "Among ourselves we have the impression that we speak as Germans to Germans— such is our impression. But though we may after all feel totally German, the others feel us to be totally un-German. We may now be called a Max Reinhardt and have inspired the [German] stage to an unanticipated revival, or, as a Hugo von Hofmannsthal, have introduced a new poetic style to replace the exhausted style of Schiller; we may call this German, but the others call it Jewish; they detect in us something 'Asiatic' and miss the German spirit *(germanische Gemut),* and should they—reluctantly—feel obliged to acknowledge our achievement, they wish we would achieve less."[9]

In an editorial presenting a selection of the ninety or so replies elicited by "The German-Jewish Parnassus"— many of which were lengthy manuscripts, mostly by Jews —the editor of *Der Kunstwart,* Ferdinand Avenarius (1856– 1923), endorsed Goldstein's sweeping characterization of the Jews' putative domination of German culture.[10] Focus-

ing on Berlin, Avenarius noted that the press was all but
a Jewish monopoly; the theatre was as well, with virtually all of the directors being Jews and as many of the
actors. He was likewise quick to agree with Goldstein that
the musical life of the German capital would be unthink-
able without the Jews.[11] As a nephew of Richard Wagner,[12]
Avenarius probably did not regard this as a laudable development. He also approvingly cited Goldstein's observation that "even the study of German literature seems to be
passing into Jewish hands . . . [and] that not a few guardians of German art realize to their chagrin how many
Jews there are among the 'German poets.' "[13] Similarly, in
amending an oversight by Goldstein, Avenarius noted that
art and art galleries in Germany were increasingly owned
by Jews.[14] Dissociating himself from antisemitism though
he did,[15] Avenarius seemed to have had no compunction in
appealing to popular stereotypes of Jews to explain their
emergence as the "administrators of German culture." Asserting that this role was ultimately a matter of power and
that "wealth is power," he proved his thesis by reminding
readers that "the best seats in the theatre, the most luxuri-
ous clothes, and the most expensive homes belong to the
Jews." He added that he had "recently heard claimed that
the luxury cars of the train from Berlin to the Riviera are
nigh-exclusively occupied by Jews."[16]

Goldstein, not wishing to pander to antisemitic sentiment, conceded at the very outset of his article that by
raising the issue in the general press he would doubtless
tap anti-Jewish feelings.[17] But he was determined to address
his fellow Literatenjuden and felt that he had no other
forum. Indeed, he turned to *Der Kunstwart*, dedicated to
neoconservative opinion,[18] only after his article was thrice
rejected as inappropriate by liberal organs.[19] Propelled by
a sense of urgency, he sought to awaken his fellow Jewish

writers from what he believed to be a dangerous compla-
cency and even a studied indifference to "the intolerable
and undignified ambiguity" of being both a German and a
Jew.[20] At the conclusion of his article he admits confusion.
"Where do we go from here?" he asks wistfully.[21] Though
drawn to Zionism, he knew he could not turn his back on
Germany and German culture: "The German spring is our
spring as the German winter is for us winter. . . . Were
we not raised on German fairy tales? Have we not played
with Little Red Ridinghood and Sleeping Beauty? Were we
not saddened for Snow White and happy with the Seven
Dwarfs? Are not the German forests alive for us? Are we
not also allowed to behold its elfs and gnomes? Do we
not understand the murmur of its streams and the song of
its birds?"[22] To deny being German would, then, be ludicrous—indeed, impossible.

Offering no solace, Goldstein settled for calling upon
his fellow Literatenjuden simply to acknowledge their dilemma. "Our worse enemy," he exclaimed, is not the antisemites[23] but rather "those Jews who continue to take part
in German culture pretending and persuading themselves
that they are not recognized. These Jews are our true ene-
mies."[24]

Among the many echoes of the *Kunstwart* debate was
a private exchange, briefly alluded to in the previous chapter, between two extraordinarily precocious twenty-year-
old students, Walter Benjamin and Ludwig Strauss.[25] The
latter, already an accomplished poet and later an eminent
scholar of German literature, had published in *Der Kunstwart* in August 1912 a long reply to Goldstein's article.[26]
After reading the reply Benjamin dashed off an enthusiastic letter to its author, dated September 1912. A brief but
intense correspondence ensued regarding the Literaten-

juden, their place in German culture, and the nature and obligations of their Jewish identity.

In the *Kunstwart* essay, Strauss, writing under the pseudonym Franz Quentin, commends Goldstein for raising the issues that he did, but faults him for emphasizing exclusively the external historical forces that kept the Jews of Germany separate. It would be more fruitful, Strauss contends, to consider the "inner structure" and "inner forces" that preserved German Jewry as a distinct entity.[27] Taking heart from the emergence of a national Jewish culture in Palestine, Strauss notes that secularization had not necessarily meant the demise of the Jewish people. With respect to Germany, he further comments that despite assimilation and the concomitant "decimation"[28] of Jewish culture, "German Jews can still be regarded as part of the Jewish people *(Volk)*."[29]

Intellectual and spiritual acculturation, Strauss observes, have proven incapable of bringing about the full assimilation of German Jewry. The persistence of antisemitism is only a partial explanation. To be sure, he continues, the encounter with German culture has given rise to a "new type" of Jew—Jews who desire to be German to the inner core of their being while retaining, often despite themselves, a distinctively Jewish sensibility.[30] Cutting deep into the primordial culture of the Jews of Germany, assimilation seems to have left untouched an impermeable core of Jewish spiritual sensibility. Strauss refers to Buber's *Drei Reden über das Judentum* (Three addresses on Judaism), published the previous year, and cites him extensively on the abiding and ever resilient "substance" of the Jewish soul.[31]

At this point, Strauss discerns a dialectic process that seems to have intrigued Benjamin. Driven to the last bas-

tion of Jewishness—the primal Jewish soul, which, one
learned from Buber, was prior to any institutional expression of Judaism—acculturated German Jews are overtaken
by an instinct for self-preservation.[32] Hence, according to
Strauss, there is now a "national" reawakening of the German Jew, a reaffirmation of the Jewish soul, and a quest to
reappropriate Jewish values.

One passage in Strauss's essay that particularly caught
Benjamin's fancy was his confession that what the enduring soul, or "essence," of the Jew is may be hard, if not
impossible, to define. But, Strauss stresses, "it is sufficient
that it be felt. However vague this feeling is, . . . it is strong,
and it is our duty to clarify it through our work."[33] This
work should be pursued through the creation of "a central
journal for Jewish literature in the German language."[34]
The proposal won the immediate and wholehearted ap-
proval of Benjamin. Strauss envisioned the proposed journal as the "gathering point" for the Jewish Renaissance, a
forum encouraging "conscious Jews to delineate the shape
(Gestalt) of the Jewish spirit clearly and credibly."[35] Further, the journal would "pose more emphatically and ines-
capably than now the great question before which contemporary German Jews stand: Are you in the first instance a
German or a Jew?"[36]

Strauss was of the opinion that Jewish affirmation required both a decision to center one's spiritual life in Judaism and a concomitant resolve to create a distinctive Jewish culture within Germany. He dismissed out of hand
the option of "hybrid individuals and culture," which he
considered inherently "flush with uncertainty and insta-
bility."[37] German Jewry, he concluded, was at a crossroads.
"Part will submerge totally among the Germans, and part
will return to a national Jewry *(nationalen Judentum)*."[38]
Alluding to the teachings of Ahad Ha'am—the Russian

Zionist who envisioned a Jewish Palestine as a "cultural center" inspiring and sustaining the crystallization of a national, secular Jewish culture in the Diaspora—Strauss entertains the possibility of a Hebrew culture developing in Germany. "The transition of German Jewry to a modern Hebrew literature is not at all inconceivable; I personally think of going that way." He hastens to add: "I will undoubtedly always have to write in the German language. It would be fatuous to deny the German language with which we are so inextricably bound."[39] (Strauss eventually made the transition to Hebrew, publishing poetry in that language—but only after his emigration to Palestine in 1935—as well as monographs, not insignificantly on German literature.)[40]

Benjamin was clearly taken by Strauss's analysis of the spiritual condition of acculturated German Jewry. In his reply to Strauss, he concurred that we are indeed "bifurcated *(zweiseitig),* Jewish and German."[41] We affirm, however, only the German side of our being, "the Jewish side having but an exotic (worse: sentimental) aroma." One should not be surprised by the asymmetry of the German-Jewish identity, Benjamin suggests, for "one could not possibly bear in one's soul both aspects of [this] bifurcated spirit in a well-balanced manner." Herein he sees the value of Strauss's proposed journal. German Jews who have perforce given priority to the German dimension of their identity will "discover" the Jewish cultural element, traces of which are presumably still hidden within their souls. In the envisioned journal, Benjamin elaborates, we will consider our bifurcated reality "from within Judaism," that is, with reference to the specifics of the German-Jewish experience. We will see that "which we have hitherto seen only with German eyes."

Benjamin was also fascinated by Strauss's conception

(again, borrowed from Buber) of Jewish spiritual life as transcending the formal boundaries of religion and as manifest in a variety of cultural expressions. More concerned with sensibility than culture in some formal ideational and institutional sense, he suggests topics that the journal should consider: "Jewish and German love," "Jews and friendship," "Jews and luxury." Benjamin was confident that by exploring such topics from a Jewish, thus unapologetic perspective, the journal would restore "self-confidence" to the German Jew and thereby help stem the tide of assimilation.

At this point in the correspondence, Benjamin expresses serious reservations concerning Strauss's Zionism. Although he concurs with Strauss's analysis of German Jewry, he questions how he could draw Zionist conclusions from it: "Wie man von hier zum Zionismus kommt, verstehe ich nicht." Zionism, he concedes, may perhaps be the only viable solution for East European Jewry. Threatened with assimilation, especially in the wake of the massive waves of emigration, East European Jewry, blessed, as he puts it, with "distinctive and most valuable forces," seemingly has little choice but to seek refuge in a Jewish state, as little choice, he suggests, as "a person fleeing a burning building." Benjamin thus tells Strauss that he will continue to pay his "shekel," his annual membership dues, to the Zionist movement. But, he maintains, Zionism is utterly irrelevant to the experience of West European Jewry. Accordingly, he finds Strauss's vision of creating in Germany an autonomous Jewish culture, beholden to a spiritual center to arise in Palestine, to be untenable and objectionable. "The best of West European Jews," he avers, "are not free *as* Jews," for they are bound to a process larger themselves.[42] "To the degree that Jews are among the scientific, literary, and commercial leadership *(Führenden),*" they are in the forefront of an "internationalism" that transcends established, parochial boundaries of knowledge and economic activity.[43] It would thus be reprehensible to remove German Jewry from this "worthy process."[44] To make his point, Benjamin cites the novelist Heinrich Mann, who rhetorically asked: "What would become of the life of the spirit, art, and love [in Germany] without the Jews?"[45]

These reservations notwithstanding, Benjamin calls himself a Zionist, but a Zionist of a special order. In deliberate contrast to the political[46] and cultural[47] Zionism centered on Palestine, Benjamin's, as he defines it, is a "Zionism of the Spirit" *(Zionismus des Geistes)*.[48] He is a Zionist, he explains, because he regards himself a *Nationaljude*,[49] as one whose Judaism is borne by a national or ethnic bond with his fellow Jews—a bond forged by shared spiritual sensibilities, independent of formal religious belief and practice. As a Zionist of the Spirit, he discerns "Jewish values everywhere"[50]—and he evidently understands "everywhere" as both a geographic and a cultural category. What may be regarded as Jewish is restricted to neither place nor what is formally held to be Judaism. Benjamin relates that he first came to this position not on the basis of a personal experience *(Erlebnis)* but because of an insight *(Erfahrung)* that it was mostly Jews who shared his intellectual and political disposition. Jews constitute "an elite in the party of intellectuals" *(Geistigen)*.[51] Apparently to indicate that this feeling is not a matter of ethnic conceit, Benjamin mentions his "extraordinary joy when [he] meets a German among the intellectuals."[52] Jewry, he continues, "is for me in no respect an end in itself, but merely the most eminent bearer and representative of matters spiritual and intellectual."[53] The fact that Jews form what Goldstein ironically called a "Parnassus" that administers German culture, Benjamin thus implies, is not a sociological fluke but a manifestation of a metaphysical destiny.

It would, therefore, violate some higher law were Jews to deny their "mission."[54]

The nature of this mission is to be understood, Benjamin argues, by examining the much maligned *Literaten*. "It is they," he insists, "who take matters of the spirit most seriously. . . ." It is they who "draw logical conclusions from our famous Enlightenment and lack of reason *(Vernunftslosigkeit).* They are not satisfied with being 'enlightened' while remaining stuck in bourgeois security."[55] By virtue of their vocation, the Literaten are "radicals."[56] Hence, their "energy,"[57] especially in politics, cannot, must not, be constrained, if they are Jews, by Judaism. As he repeats throughout the correspondence with Strauss, "an individual can have only one *Schwerpunkt"*—one focal point for his or her energy.[58]

For the Zionists of the Spirit, then, Judaism must remain "thoroughly esoteric."[59] Hence, it must remain vague. Benjamin puts it paradoxically: ill defined but self-understood. Just as morality is said to "understand itself by itself," he claims, "so Judaism must understand itself by itself,"[60] that is, intuitively without any external instruction, doctrinal catechisms, or theological guidance. And with a sudden gravity, he adds, "To my mind, all that is Jewish which seeks to go beyond the self-understood is dangerous."[61] The danger, typical of all ideologies, indeed, all fixed ideational systems, is the deadening of all that is vital and creative.[62]

Judaism, at least for the Literatenjuden, must remain an implicit aspect of one's being; it must remain an esoteric *Gesinnung,* or disposition, never to cross the threshold between a hidden sensibility and a realm of explicit declarations and affiliation. Benjamin accordingly tells Strauss that he cannot place Judaism—"which I acknowledge and love"[63]—at the center of his intellectual and political life.

The only explicit expression of Judaism that he would allow is the journal proposed by Strauss. As a forum for Jewish self-reflection and exploration, the journal would strengthen the self-esteem of its readers—Benjamin presumably again has in mind his fellow Literatenjuden, who, fortified by the journal, would resume with a secret pride their work in a world that inevitably misunderstands them. Apparently prodded by Strauss to spell out this work and explain how it may be construed as Jewish, Benjamin replied with a parable. He relates his vision of an "esoteric" *Kulturjudentum* to a rereading of the story of the Tower of Babel. The activity of this esoteric, "subterranean"[64] Judaism is that of "a reverse Tower of Babel. The people of the Bible heaped building blocks upon building blocks, but the object of their spiritual will—a tower soaring up into heaven—did not arise. [In contrast, contemporary] Jews[65] wield ideas as building blocks, and never will they reach the origin [*Ursprung*] of all: matter. They build from above without [ever] reaching the ground."[66] So concludes Benjamin's presentation of an avowedly idiosyncratic view of Zionism and Judaism.

Strauss's letters in reply to Benjamin are not extant. One may surmise that he firmly adhered to an exoteric Zionism of explicit Jewish deeds and to his conviction, expressed at the conclusion of his *Kunstwart* essay, that "so long as the Jewish element dominates [one's bifurcated soul] it will belong to the center of our lives and creativity . . . , [allowing us] to become something whole."[67]

With the close of their intense six-month correspondence,[68] Benjamin's and Strauss's paths never again crossed except indirectly. In 1929 Strauss earned his doctorate at the University of Frankfurt with a dissertation on Hölderlin,[69] which he wrote under the supervision of the same professor—Franz Schultz—who a few years earlier had rejected Benjamin's *Habilitationsschrift* on the origin of German tragic drama.[70]

Strauss never published his journal. He did, however, take an active role in a variety of Jewish journals, especially in *Der Jude*, founded by his future father-in-law, Martin Buber, in 1916.[71] The very name of Buber's journal, which soon became one of the foremost literary and political reviews of its day, highlighted a profound change in Jewish self-consciousness. Just a generation earlier, the term *Jude* (Jew) had often evoked shame and embarrassment among German-speaking Jews. As a young university student, Buber himself had hesitated to utter the word "Jew" in public, for in cultured circles it was considered somewhat of an obscenity.[72] To publish less than twenty years later a journal with the words "Der Jude" emblazoned on its masthead was thus nothing short of revolutionary. Founded during the First World War, when there was a disturbing intensification of antisemitism, the journal was surely an expression of defiant pride. But it was more than that. As Arthur A. Cohen notes in the introduction to the volume of translated selections from *Der Jude*, which he edited: "[C]alling the periodical *The Jew* . . . says something about its audience as well as about its [editor]. It would be hard to imagine the postman dropping such a periodical into the mailboxes of American Jews. Yet in Berlin, Vienna, Prague . . . there arrived with relative punctuality each month between April 1916 and 1923 (and irregularly thereafter), wrapped but not concealed, the periodical *The Jew*."[73] The pride—the readiness to be identified as Jews—was surely more than spite, what was popularly called *Trotzjudentum*, "a Judaism out of defiance," or what Theodor Herzl (1870–1904), the founding father of political Zionism, called a negative pride: Jewish self-assertion to spite the antisemites.

To be sure, a renewed sense of Jewish solidarity in the face of heightened bigotry played a role in the shaping of the consciousness of Buber's audience.[74] But the resurgence of Jewish pride was also primed by "positive" forces inherent in the development of German-Jewish history and identity. The Israeli historian Shulamit Volkov has decisively shown that since the very beginnings of modern German-Jewish history there has been a unique dialectical interrelation between assimilation and dissimilation.[75] Examining "the inner dynamics of assimilation itself," Volkov discerns various social and psychological forces that have often led acculturated German Jews to halt at the edge of total assimilation and reassess and revitalize their relation to Judaism. Beginning in the 1890s, Volkov notes, this tendency became a distinct trend. Dissimilation was, in a sense, a dialectical spin-off of the success of assimilation. With particular reference to the generation that came to maturity just before or during the world war, Volkov observes: "A generation of Jews [emerged], who, relatively free from the anxiety of social climbing, were beginning to look inward. . . . It was for many of them a matter of reaching the limits of assimilation and promptly halting at the brink. From that point one could only turn backward and inward, seeking a new definition of one's identity, and often also a new self-respect."[76] The mood of this generation was captured by the philosopher Ernst Bloch, who in 1912, upon reading a volume of Buber's hasidic stories, exulted, "The pride of being Jewish is reawakened!" *(Neu erwacht der Stolz, jüdisch zu sein!)*.[77]

Even as early as 1900 it was possible to speak of a Jewish Renaissance in Germany.[78] Inspired in part by Zionism, Jewish culture burgeoned. Let me mention a few of the artists, mostly centered in Berlin, who adapted Jewish themes to their work at the turn of the century: Joseph

Budko (1888–1940), E. M. Lilien (1874–1924), Karl Schwarz (1885–1962), Hermann Struck (1876–1944), and Lesser Ury (1861–1931).[79] Much of their work was in the illustration of the many books and periodicals of Jewish interest that appeared in the years before the world war. Although not all of these artists were from assimilated German-Jewish backgrounds, their audience was overwhelmingly so.

The dynamic and youthful leader of the German Zionist Federation, Kurt Blumenfeld (1884–1963), spoke in 1908 of a revolution that he hailed as "postassimilation Zionism."[80] The phrase was immediately adopted by his contemporaries as a programmatic slogan and, indeed, was expanded to refer to a postassimilatory Judaism in general.[81] The shift in German-Jewish consciousness was hardly as revolutionary as Blumenfeld had envisioned. As the Czech Zioinist Shmuel Hugo Bergmann (1883–1975) complained in a letter to Buber, the so-called German-Jewish Renaissance was nearly exclusively "literary"; it was, in his sarcastic words, a "Judaism of speeches."[82]

Though substantially correct in his assessment, Bergmann overstates his case. There were some, though relatively few, determined efforts to go beyond declaratory and sentimental expressions of Jewishness and to reappropriate Jewish knowledge. Still others, like Franz Rosenzweig, sought to reclaim the life of traditional Jewish religious practice. It is perhaps apposite to note that Rosenzweig's spiritual quest, culminating in his affirmation of Judaism, was not in any significant way prompted by antisemitism.

The world war—with the attendant antisemitism,[83] particularly the encounter with the East European Jewish masses[84]—contributed enormously to the process of returning erstwhile assimilated Jews to an affirmative Jewishness. Let us not exaggerate; we are still speaking of a minority, but an ever growing and vibrant one.[85] The deep-

ening of Jewish consciousness and commitment did not
undermine or attenuate the attachment to German culture, however. Blumenfeld, in his youthful exuberance,
had called upon German Jewry to reverse the humilia-
tion of assimilation by extirpating themselves from German culture; yet he, too, could not disengage himself from
the literature, the music, and especially the language that
he had learned to love.[86] Ernst Bloch described the situation with a simple elegance. After joyously acclaiming the
newly found pride in Judaism, a sentiment cited above,
he says: "[This pride] stirs in us restlessly, but we remain
mixed and ambiguous [gemischt und zweideutig]."[87]

The rediscovery and reaffirmation of Judaism did not
lead in most cases to a jettisoning of German and European culture. As Benjamin declared, "We are bifurcated
—Jewish and German." The relation between these two
components of individual identity became the passionate
preoccupation of German Jewry.

The Benjamin-Strauss correspondence illustrates the
torment aroused by and depths plumbed in discussions of
the German Jew's divided soul. But it was the great neo-
Kantian philosopher Hermann Cohen (1842–1918) who
paradoxically raised the German-Jewish dilemma to a new
level of discourse. On the one hand, he presented a beguilingly irenic view of a German-Jewish symbiosis, and, on
the other, he implicitly illuminated the problematic nature
of this relationship.

It was Hermann Cohen, as Leo Strauss remarked, who
"symbolized more than anyone else the union of Jewish
faith and German culture."[88] During the world war he published two identically entitled essays: "Deutschtum und
Judentum."[89] The title more than the content of the essays
gave a special impetus to the debate that so exercised postassimilatory Jewry. As I shall consider more extensively

in the next chapter, the title of Cohen's seminal essay
focused the debate on the "and," the dialectics of that not
so innocent conjunction linking Jewish loyalties and German culture. With a subtlety becoming a transcendental
philosopher, Cohen problematized the "and," which otherwise might be regarded as a simple particle of speech.

With broad, sweeping strokes and without any apparent irony, Cohen assumes in the essays a parity, an inherent compatibility and complementarity, between Judaism
and German culture, or, more precisely, between the Jewish and German ethos: "We German Jews . . . derive a sense
of the closest religious communion from the accord exist-
ing between Jewish messianism and German humanism.
Our feeling for Germany and its people has therefore religious overtones, so to speak, and is marked by a sense of
religious affirmation. In perfect equanimity and harmony
of soul, we feel as secure in our German patriotism as in
our Jewish religion."[90] In light of such pronouncements,
Cohen has been branded naive and pilloried for fostering
the "delusion" of a German-Jewish symbiosis that proved
so tragically dangerous.[91]

But Cohen was hardly naive and benighted. He has to
be read with all the Kantian inflections that he intended.
Read that way, there is a great deal of irony — and anguish —
between the lines. As the late Steven S. Schwarzschild
has reminded us, Cohen was fiercely anti-Hegelian and
deemed it as both philosophically inane and politically re-
actionary to view, as Hegel had, the real, empirical world
as rational.[92] There is, Cohen averred, a "world of difference between Kant and Hegel," for, as Cohen paraphrases
him, the sage of Königsberg would say, "What is rational is
not actual but ought to become."[93]

What Cohen proffered is, accordingly, an ideal construct meant to disclose the shortcomings of the present

reality. Holding up the ideal as a mirror, he sought ever so gently to rebuke contemporary Germans and prod them to heed their humanistic heritage. Writing his essays on Deutschtum and Judentum in the midst of the world war, he disregarded the mounting accusations of Jewish disloyalty and the nervous presence of the military censors and warned Germany against the dangers of imperialistic nationalism: "To ensure the ethical conduct of its religious and public affairs, Germany must realize that nothing will endanger and corrupt a people more than its attempt to play providence even with regard to politics. No political self-interest, neither immediate nor long range, entitles a people to decide whether another people or nationality has a right to live. And if this is true in the realm of politics, it is equally true in the realm of religion."[94]

Speaking of the noumenal or ideal Germany, Cohen thus spoke indirectly and critically of the empirical Germany. Earlier, in 1907, he had acknowledged en passant in the preface to a philosophical work on ethics that his views differed from those of the modern "style of *Deutschtum.*" He had added that he took heart from the knowledge that an alternative tradition informs the "German spirit," which, braced with its "original power," will ultimately prevail over its "ephemeral distortions."[95]

In the first of his "Deutschtum und Judentum" essays Cohen contends that the authentic German spirit requires that "every German individual must know his Schiller and his Goethe with the intimacy *(Innigkeit)* of love and bear them in his spirit and heart. This intimacy presupposes, however, that he has also attained a popular but scientifically sound *(Volkswissenschaftliche)* insight into and knowledge of his Kant."[96] He goes on to expound on Kant's vision of eternal peace. In the same context, he also states parenthetically that "hatred is not a serious emotion in the German soul" *(der Haß ist kein ernsthafter Affekt in der deutschen Seele).*[97] I imagine that many of Cohen's contemporary readers would have responded to such statements with expletives or a muffled sigh: "Who is he kidding?" Cohen may have anticipated, even desired, such a response. Again, we must recall that he wrote this essay in the early years of the war, when jingoism was at its height and the German hit parade included such ballads as "Song of Hate Against England"—incidentally written by a Jew, Ernst Lissauer,[98] who was also one of the participants in the *Kunstwart* debate.[99]

In a postscript to the first version of "Deutschtum und Judentum" written in 1916—when the infamous *Judenzählung,* the census of Jews in combat units to determine whether they were shirking their national responsibility, was being conducted—Cohen declares his confidence that the German people will ultimately affirm their pristine humanist, cosmopolitan vocation.[100] It is inconceivable, he continues, that such a Germany would "demand of me that I surrender my religion and religious inheritance." There was no talk then in Germany of denying the Jews the right to practice their ancestral faith; but he chose this patently false issue to defend obliquely the integrity of the Jews of Germany and also undoubtedly to fortify the spirit of his fellow Jews in the face of outright antisemitic slander. Accordingly, in the peroration of the second version of "Deutschtum und Judentum," he offers a vision: "There has never been a dearth of German individuals who have been fond of and have put their trust in their German Jews. Maybe—who can foretell the course of history?—it will one day be considered not among the least of its glories that Germany not only granted protective and civil rights to its Jews but also made them part of that spirit which informs German science, German art, and all other expressions of German creativity; that it lent its most sympathetic support to the cultivation of the Jewish religion to the benefit of the entire world; and that it paved the way for the attainment of a spiritual harmony between German and Jew on a level probably unmatched in the modern world—a harmony for which the Jew, to be sure, owes the greater debt of gratitude."[101] In this vision one detects wistfulness—"who can foretell the course of history?"—rather than prophetic certainty. Cohen is not describing the empirical Germany but offering a guarded hope that the German-Jewish Parnassus—that is, the Jews' embrace of German culture—will no longer be a cause of resentment, but a cause of pride.

Cohen died in April 1918, less than a year before the proclamation of the Weimar Republic. He surely would have been overjoyed that the republic had consciously associated itself, albeit not by intent, with the seat and thus heritage of German classical humanism.[102] He would have also felt vindicated that the new republic was, as the German title of Peter Gay's magisterial study of Weimar culture[103] has it, a "Republik der Außenseiter" (republic of outsiders),[104] which welcomed former outsiders to participate in all aspects of the country's political and cultural life. It was indeed the coming of age of the German-Jewish Parnassus. Cohen would also have been particularly pleased that the republic created the climate for an unprecedented flourishing of Jewish culture.[105] If before the war there were the beginnings of a postassimilatory Jewish Renaissance in Germany, now it was in full bloom. The sweet fragrance of renewal touched virtually every aspect of Jewish life in Weimar Germany. New and serious journals on Jewish affairs sprang up; Jewish academic scholarship reached un-

precedented heights; Jewish theology and philosophy attained a new vitality, initiated by the publication in 1919
of Cohen's posthumous work, *Religion of Reason out of
the Sources of Judaism*.[106] But the hallmark of the period
was undoubtedly the rebirth of popular Jewish learning
and Torah study, focused in the person and educational activities of Cohen's disciple and friend Franz Rosenzweig.[107]

Rosenzweig spoke, as already noted, of a New Babylon—a Zweistromland,[108] a land fecundated by the convergence of two vital sources: a Jewry nurtured by German
culture—or, rather, universal culture refracted through the
German experience and imagination—and the traditional
religious wisdom and spirituality of Israel. For a brief moment it seemed that Germany might, indeed, become a
New Babylon. Unlike the Babylon of yore, whose aca-
demies of Jewish learning survived for many centuries,
tragedy befell the German-Jewish Babylon after less than
fifteen years. Classical Babylonian Jewry secured the foun-
dations upon which traditional Judaism still stands, and
Jewry continues to be beholden to the legacy of those who
dwelt between the Tigris and the Euphrates. In contrast,
the legacy of the German-Jewish Babylon is flush with
ambiguity. In the Epilogue, I reflect on the ambiguities of
the German-Jewish legacy and insist that they must be
ultimately assessed in the light of the vision of a New
Babylon animated, as it was, by a resolve to affirm Judaism
as a vital spiritual reality while maintaining a passionate
engagement in modern, humanistic culture.

I would like to conclude this chapter with two poems
by Rosenzweig's first mentor in Talmud, Rabbi Nehemiah Nobel. A traditional rabbi with a keen interest in
German letters and philosophy, Nobel wrote the German
and Hebrew inscriptions for the tombstone of Hermann
Cohen. In translation the German inscription reads:

Plato's radiant world and Kant's
awing profundity
Radiate in you, O Master, as muses in
tune lamenting.
Ardor of the prophets did kindle the
glow of your blazing torch.
Buried here are but mortal remains. Glow
ever brighter, O torch![109]

The Hebrew inscription reads:

A glorious trial! You will not be silenced,
for you inquired of sublimities.
For the sake of the remnant of Israel
you girded the remnant of your strength.
And you were to the remnant an eye
illuminating the mist,
And you removed stumbling blocks and
offences of the heart[110]
To lift up the humiliated.[111]

Chapter Four

Franz Rosenzweig's Eulogy for German Jewry

Franz Rosenzweig did not write a eulogy for German Jewry. He died in December 1929, three years before Hitler seized the reins of government; and when, after a long illness, he passed away, just two weeks shy of his forty-third birthday, he was full of hope for the vibrant future of German Jewry, which was then in the midst of a spiritual and cultural renaissance.[1] He had become the focus and symbol of this unanticipated renewal of a Jewry that had seemed to be well on the way to self-liquidation through assimilation and spiritual atrophy. He himself had contemplated conversion to Christianity, but at the foot of the baptismal font, he hesitated, and eventually he affirmed Judaism as a religious reality deserving the passionate attention of fellow Jews who, like himself, as denizens of a world of bourgeois ambition and culture, were estranged from the Torah and its teachings. Singularly identified with the renaissance of German Jewry, which coincided with the tragically brief years of the Weimar Republic, Rosenzweig's life and thought may be said to have constituted a summary—a dialectical gathering—of the forces, the energies and passions, that shaped German-Jewish history.

As Rabbi Leo Baeck observed, Rosenzweig was "a child of the Jewish Renaissance. As it happened to him, so it happened to others. But to him was given what God gives

66

to few: to tell what he experienced, and say what it meant to him."[2] Rosenzweig was, in fact, keenly aware that he was destined to serve as the amanuensis of his generation and to articulate the common experience, which, he held, signified German Jewry's coming of age. Blessed with an acute historical consciousness, which was nurtured by his study of Hegel,[3] he had a nuanced appreciation of the dialectical thrust of German-Jewish history as it unfolded from the time of Mendelssohn to his own generation—a generation that, he held, witnessed the maturing promise and, paradoxically, the increasingly manifest limitations of Israel's romance with Deutschtum, the alluring realm of German language and culture. The acknowledgment of both the promise and limitations of the Jews' relationship with Deutschtum—and European culture in general—he contended, was at the heart of the Jewish Renaissance.

Rosenzweig belonged to a family that cultivated a proud consciousness of their genealogy and regarded their chain of illustrious ancestors as marking, in microcosm, the fortunes of German-Jewish history. Even as a young man, Rosenzweig saw his family history as representative of the spiritual biography of German Jewry. The family's origins could be traced back to Mordecai Jaffe,[4] one of the leading Talmudists and kabbalists of the sixteenth century, and to the legendary Maharal of Prague,[5] placing Rosenzweig's family among the "spiritual aristocracy" of Central European Jewry. His great-grandfather, Samuel Meyer Ehrenberg (1773–1853), was one of the transitional figures in the move from the Ghetto to the Enlightenment.[6] He was the headmaster of the Samsonschule—the Jewish Free School of Wolfenbüttel—which pioneered a modern, secular education for Jewish youth.[7] Inspired by the promise of Jewish Emancipation, the school, under Ehrenberg's tutelage, abandoned the traditional curriculum of a *talmud torah* and, as Ehrenberg put it, set out "to transform ignorant, ill-bred *bachurim*, crude in speech and ideas, into well-bred, polished young men."[8] Ehrenberg counted among his pupils Isaac Marcus Jost (1793–1860) and Leopold Zunz (1794–1886), the fathers of modern Jewish studies.[9]

Zunz, in particular, remained close to his beloved teacher, even extending his affection to members of Ehrenberg's family. Rosenzweig's favorite aunt, *Grosstante* Julie Ehrenberg, who died in her mid-nineties full of charm and intellectual vigor, was one of Zunz's closest companions, and her reminiscences of the great scholar helped ensure his place as a sort of "family saint."[10] With the blessings of Samuel Meyer Ehrenberg, Zunz initiated the study of Jewish texts according to the criteria of modern, scientific scholarship and placed the investigation of the Jewish past in a firm historicist mold. In his very first essay, "Etwas über die rabbinische Literatur," he coolly and unremorsefully declared that with the Jews' embrace of modern culture, traditional Jewish learning and creativity had come to an end.[11] Accordingly, he somberly noted that now that Judaism was "being carried to its grave,"[12] it was appropriate to honor its memory with a judicious and dignified evaluation of its varied spiritual and intellectual achievements. Scholars of Judaism would have the solemn task of writing a balanced obituary for the erstwhile civilization of the Jews. Writing in 1818, Zunz observed with the studied detachment of a modern scholar that "precisely because Jews in our times—limiting our attention to the Jews of Germany—are seizing upon the German language and German learning [*Bildung*] with such earnestness and are thus, unwittingly, carrying [rabbinic literature] to its grave, scientific scholarship steps in demanding an account of what has already been sealed away."[13] This task took on urgency because it was certain that within a century—

"by 1919"—no Hebrew books would be available; that is, by 1919 Jews would have ceased to revere this literature, and no one would be capable of properly evaluating it.[14] The year 1919 was, as it turned out, the year in which Rosenzweig completed his great philosophical affirmation of Judaism, *The Star of Redemption,* and resolved to commit his life to the service of the Jewish community and to the renewal of Jewish learning and creativity, a revival firmly grounded in a knowledge of the traditional Hebrew sources.

Zunz anticipated the demise of Jewish learning because, as he noted, with the Enlightenment and Emancipation, Jews had enthusiastically rushed to drink of the waters of German Kultur. When he wrote his prognosis in 1818, the twenty-four-year-old Zunz shared the exuberant confidence that Jewry's adoption of the German language and culture would enhance both their personal dignity and their civil status. A century later, looking back at the Jews' romance with Deutschtum, Rosenzweig was aware that the results were often ambiguous. He gave a case in point. The fact, he explained, that Jews now sought their intellectual and spiritual sustenance beyond the precincts of Judaism led not only to the eclipse of traditional Jewish learning and culture but also to the thinning of the social fabric of Jewish life. In his own family, despite the carefully cultivated pride of pedigree,[15] conversions were many. In his generation one of his closest cousins, Hans Ehrenberg (1883–1958)—the son of his father's first cousin—converted to Christianity, later becoming a prominent Lutheran pastor.[16] The irony of the many converts in this family, one of the pillars of German Jewry, was captured by another of Rosenzweig's cousins, Rudolf (Rudi) Ehrenberg (1884–1969), whose father, Victor Ehrenberg (1851–1929), a renowned professor of law at the University of Leipzig, had converted to Christianity upon marrying a non-Jewish woman. Victor's wife, Helene von Ihering (1852–1920), was a direct descendant of Martin Luther.[17] In her care was placed the wedding gown worn by Luther's bride, the former Cistercian nun Catherine von Bora.[18] Thus Rudi, Rosenzweig's beloved cousin, could trace his ancestry on his father's side to the Maharal of Prague and on his mother's to Martin Luther.

A noble lineage, but deriving from two opposing spiritual estates, it left Rudi—so he felt—bereft of title and patrimony. A descendant of two distinguished spiritual aristocracies, he was heir to neither tradition and was thus a spiritual déclassé. On the occasion of a speech he gave at Rosenzweig's wedding,[19] in March 1920, he alluded to his dual pedigree as it reflected his loss of all spiritual nobility —a condition, he suggested, that was shared by his family and all Jews since they left the ghetto and came to subscribe to the bourgeois creed of progress and an epicurean pursuit of well-being. The family's effort to retain a semblance of tradition by ceremonial expressions of familial sentiments and fidelity were, Rudi declared, inherently incapable of preserving the power and nobility of a venerable tradition.

These reflections were woven into Rudi's toast to his cousin and closest friend Franz[20] and his bride, Edith. The presentation of a toast was a family custom established by Samuel Meyer Ehrenberg.[21] Upon Ehrenberg's twenty-fifth anniversary as the headmaster of the Samsonschule, his students, including Jost and Zunz, gave him a specially crafted ceremonial silver goblet.[22] In his last will and testament, Ehrenberg charged that this goblet be used at family weddings to toast the nuptials, and the goblet was passed from generation to generation.[23] In making the traditional family toast, Rudi raised the vessel bequeathed by

his and Franz's common great-grandfather and noted that
"he who gave this goblet was still himself just out of the
ghetto; his great-grandson, who today passes on the goblet,
is half Christian and half Jew."[24] But, Rudi asked, can the
unique tradition of a Jewish family have meaning when
the Jewish tradition at large has been relinquished? Can
a Jewish family aspire to nobility solely on the basis of a
ritual inspired by sentiment and devoid of genuine tradition? Undoubtedly, "for a good noble family tradition is
self-evident—the very notion of nobility, knightly honor,
fidelity to the monarch, et cetera." But it is manifestly
otherwise, he continued, with emancipated, western Jewish families and, in fact, for all who had been seduced by
the secular myths of the nineteenth century.

The toasts that he had heard on previous family occa-
sions, Rudi continued, "tended to praise and express a
desire for the firm cohesion of the family." The cohesion sought after was, however, "horizontal." The aristocratic conception of a "longitudinal" family tradition had
long eluded the Ehrenberg and Rosenzweig families. Rudi
mournfully acknowledged that a longitudinal tradition
"was not in accord with the time and its spirit. Like all
aristocracy, like all unique traditions, the aristocratic conception became bloodless, tepid—so must it be ever more
so with a Jewish family whose descendants, from father to
son, each represent a further subtraction from the Jewish
way of life."

Hence, Rudi mused, it was perhaps not coincidental
that since the Revolution that buffeted Germany in the
wake of the world war—which marked the end of the bourgeois illusions of the nineteenth century, both political
and cultural—it was no longer the fathers but the sons of
the family who assumed the family ritual of the wedding
toast. It was Franz himself who first broke the family tradi-

tion. On the occasion of another cousin's wedding, in April 1919,[25] the toast was made by him rather than the father of the groom, as prescribed by family custom. "When Franz's and my great-grandfather gave this wedding goblet," Rudi noted, "he wanted it to inspire on this festive occasion a word from the fathers to the sons, and thus it had been through the generations."

But since the Revolution, the blessing of fathers had been replaced by that of brothers.[26] "The Revolution only rendered the cleavage [between father and son] that much more apparent, made it manifest to all. Our fathers contended that we are the ones who severed the chain of the generations, that we are the rebels against the tradition. . . . But is that really so? Are we the believers in progress, the prophets of [inexorable] development? Are we the votaries of the Enlightenment, who have felt themselves to have outgrown the naive faith of their fathers? No, we are not. We are the sons of our fathers only because we once again wish to be grandchildren—great-grandsons and authentic descendants. Our fathers saw the cleavage before them, because their eyes looked only forward, and not back. We, however, believe that one can proceed forward if—and only if—one first receives." Rudi was obliquely referring to his generation's quest to reclaim the spiritual patrimony that was lost through the withering of tradition. This generation often longingly called this quest a "homeward" journey.

Concluding his toast, Rudi turned to his cousin and his bride and exclaimed, "Franz and Edith, you both have returned home to the house of your forefathers, but not without struggle and pain. If ever a festivity was in order, [it is today,] and so it is today that the token of ancestral love that is this goblet is given to you." Rudi added, "I must admit that for me, whose existence is a product of estrangement from tradition, it was a bit strange when

suddenly the old Samuel Meyer appeared with his goblet
at my wedding.[27] I clearly have less right to it than you."

In contrast to himself, Rudi claimed, for Edith and Franz
the goblet could have abundant meaning. Samuel Meyer
Ehrenberg had in his last will and testament expressed the
hope that the goblet—a Jewish vessel—would be filled with
German wine. As Rudi explained: "This goblet, presented
to an old Jewish master by his Jewish students, when filled
with German wine can for you become a genuine symbol:
the Jewish goblet—a vessel, metal, form—all that endures,
what the Jews call tradition," and German wine, "the ever
changing contents, the living waters that mature in the
glow of these days." In these closing words of his wedding
toast, Rudi was alluding to the most exigent issue now
faced by Franz, who was determined to repossess the faith
of his ancestors: namely, how to continue to drink German wine while holding firmly onto the venerable vessel
of Jewish tradition. Rudi, incidentally, eventually found
his way "home" to Christianity—into which he was bap-
tized as a child; he said that Rosenzweig's faith had helped
him understand his own.[28]

Samuel Meyer Ehrenberg, who coined the image of German wine and a Jewish goblet, died in 1853 at the age of
eighty, an observant Jew thoroughly inebriated on German
wine; that is, he rejoiced in the opportunity provided by
Deutschtum to participate in the adventure of modern culture. He employed the image of German wine and a Jewish
goblet to celebrate what undoubtedly seemed to him an un-
problematic meeting of Judentum and Deutschtum. With
exuberance he encouraged his family and students to join
the ranks of the bold new breed that emerged with the Enlightenment: the German Jew. Samuel Meyer Ehrenberg's
great-grandson Franz Rosenzweig viewed this marriage of
Judentum and Deutschtum with circumspection. He did

not object to the marriage itself, but to the *ketubah*—to the conditions specified in the marriage agreement. These conditions, he believed, would have to be more carefully worked out than those contracted by the generation that initiated the relationship.

Historically and symbolically, the marriage between Judentum and Deutschtum was initially represented by the friendship between Moses Mendelssohn and Ephraim Gotthold Lessing, a friendship immortalized in Lessing's play of 1779, *Nathan the Wise*. This allegorical drama was destined to become the emblem of the German Enlightenment and German-Jewish hopes. It served to define the horizons of the Jews' conception of their relationship with the German people and culture. Rosenzweig, however, irreverently held the play to be burdened by a benighted vision of the fraternity between German and Jew; it beguilingly suggests, he said, that goodwill and an enlightened culture alone will be sufficient to neutralize the possible sting associated with any abiding religious and cultural differences.[29] Indicatively, as Rosenzweig noted, at a climactic moment in the play Nathan plaintively protests, "Is a Christian or a Jew sooner a Christian or a Jew than a human being?"[30] To conform with the sentiments inspiring this, Rosenzweig commented, Lessing's Nathan is a disembodied Jew, "abstracted" from the concrete reality of Judaism.[31]

Nathan is, in fact, "a naked man."[32] Hence, the differences between him and members of other faith communities are "merely a matter of dress, food, and drink."[33] Rosenzweig deemed this to be a superficial and misconceived conception of tolerance, which he traced to Lessing's and Mendelssohn's "messianic" evaluation of their friendship, celebrated by them as a meeting between "pure" human beings.[34] Lessing's Nathan is truly both a pure human being and "the first German Jew."[35] To this as-

sessment Rosenzweig made an addendum, saying, with a
tinge of irony, "Of all people, the Jew was to become a pure
human being," and he alone.[36] Thus, "Mendelssohn and
Lessing are the tragedy of the Jews until this very day."[37]
Their "friendship was too messianic";[38] it was beyond history, for, as was pointed out earlier, at the conclusion of
Nathan the Wise, there are "no children."[39]

Nonetheless, Rosenzweig was quick to acknowledge
Mendelssohn's historical significance. The Jewish sage,
whose contribution to German letters and philosophy
earned for him, as previously noted, the affectionate title
of "the German Socrates," set in motion the realignment
of Jewry with world culture. Rosenzweig held that, before
Mendelssohn, the relation between Jewry and world culture was implicit and covert. Mendelssohn brought the
relation into the open, allowing it to grow and gain in fullness. It is in this sense that Mendelssohn is to be hailed
as the first German Jew; he was the first to bear "both
words"—German and Jew—"with all the weight and responsible meaning . . . which we German Jews have come
to understand by our *Deutschjudentum.*"[40] The axis of this
dual responsibility to one's primordial identity and one's
newly affirmed affiliation with Deutschtum, according to
Rosenzweig, rests in the conjunction "and." The dialectics
of German-Jewish spiritual history will be determined by
this "and"—for although a simple particle of speech, this
conjunction is not unambiguous; it signifies connection,
but its valence and semantic range may vary significantly.

As Rosenzweig observed, for Mendelssohn the "and"
served to designate a weak linkage between two separate
realities. The "and" between Judentum and Deutschtum
did not suggest to him any coordination, or covalence. One
may be Jewish, Mendelssohn argued, and also an adherent
of high culture—in his case, a proponent of German let-

ters and philosophy. The two spheres of activity, Mendelssohn asserted, are distinct and separate. Judaism, he held,
is principally a matter of obedience to a divinely revealed
law, which governs primarily the ritual life of the Jew.
The Torah teaches no truths that might conflict with the
precepts of reason, and Judaism therefore need not inter-
fere with the Jew's participation in a culture, such as that
sponsored by Deutschtum, dedicated to truth.[41] This dif-
ferentiation between Judaism, as obedience to a revealed
law, albeit grounded in ultimate truth, and culture, as the
venue for the rational acquisition of truth, had, in Rosenzweig's judgment, eliminated the metaphysical and epistemological distinctiveness of Judaism.

Rosenzweig was aware that Mendelssohn merely
sought to argue that intellectually and spiritually the Jew
is preeminently a "human being" *(Mensch)* and that he can
therefore participate qua human being in enlightened culture unencumbered by any doctrinal or cognitive demands
peculiar to Judaism. But here is the rub. According to his
own admission, Mendelssohn himself was not "a unified
human being," as Rosenzweig put it.[42] The Jew and the
human being resided in him not as an integrated whole but
next to one another *(nebeneinander)* as discrete entities.
He was both Jew *and* a human being, or rather a human
being who had attained enlightened culture. It was not
surprising that Mendelssohn's contemporaries found him
"incomprehensible."[43] As Rosenzweig rhetorically asked,
How were "they to grasp that there stood before them not
one person but two?"[44]

Mendelssohn's radical bifurcation of Judaism and cognitive culture, Rosenzweig noted, had sorrowful conse-
quences for German Jewry. It suggested that intellectual
and spiritual sustenance is to be sought, if not exclusively,
certainly primarily in Deutschtum as the domain of truth

and ethical, aesthetic, and philosophical values. But deprived of a unique claim to truth, Rosenzweig averred, Judaism must fail to engage the mind and soul of the modern Jew.

Recognizing this danger, Liberal or Reform Judaism, which emerged in the generation subsequent to Mendelssohn's, sought to balance the relation between Judentum and Deutschtum. The "and" would now designate a "together with," a partnership.[45] The various formulations of the Liberal position, as I already had occasion to observe, found their most sustained articulation in Hermann Cohen's equation of Jewish messianism and German humanism as represented by Kant and Schiller.[46] Cohen, the venerated neo-Kantian philosopher, taught that both Judentum and Deutschtum, in their most elevated expressions, promoted a common conception of humanity and of human beings' ethical duties and hopes.

Rosenzweig, despite his friendship and personal esteem for Cohen, regarded his position as sociologically and philosophically naive. Though appreciating Cohen's attempt to restore a metaphysical dignity to Judaism, Rosenzweig deemed his conception of the harmony between Judentum and Deutschtum to reflect a self-deceiving fantasy. To be sure, as Rosenzweig told his parents, who had then recently hosted Cohen in their home, the fantasy was shared by most "cultured" German Jews like themselves: "Basically it is for [Cohen] exactly as it is for you. If you wish to feel German, you associate yourselves with the small number of Germans who will regard you as such; and they are (1) Germans who are in the same situation as you, namely, other Jews; (2) some déclassé people and bohemians; (3) some doctrinaire liberals and people of goodwill; (4) converts to Judaism; and (5) those who are dependent upon you."[47]

The only difference between Cohen and themselves, he explains to his parents, is that Cohen's claim to belong to Deutschtum is even more "crass" than theirs, precisely because it is "purely intellectual."[48] Cohen factors out of Deutschtum "all but his philosophy in order to be able to present it as supreme evidence of what he means by *Deutschtum*."[49] By virtue of such a procedure, "it is easy for him [Cohen] to regard himself as a better German than the Germans themselves. For a Cohenian is naturally a better German. This infinite *chutzpah* is inherent to Cohen's very argument."[50] Rosenzweig was aware that by demonstrating the affinity of Judaism to an admittedly idealized conception of Deutschtum, Cohen was offering a sophisticated response to the charge of German antisemites that the Jews lack sufficient patriotism.[51] Nonetheless, Rosenzweig felt that Cohen's equation of Judentum and Deutschtum was both specious and disingenuous.

To be a German, Rosenzweig held, "means to assume responsibility for the entire people, to harmonize oneself not only with Goethe, Schiller, and Kant but also with the other Germans, especially with the lower classes and the middling Germans—with lowly civil servants *(Assessors)*, members of student dueling fraternities, petty clerks, pigheaded farmers, and stiff high-school teachers. The real German must include all these in his heart or suffer because of them. He can, however, ignore the average Frenchman."[52] The truth, Rosenzweig continued, is that the Jews' devotion to high culture is not to Deutschtum but to European culture. Indeed, "Cohen confounds what he as a European finds in *Deutschtum* and what the German finds therein." Surely, "German philosophy and music are European phenomena, but so are French painting and English politics, as well as the Russian novel and religiosity."[53] In comparison to Russian piety, he adds, "German piety seems as pitiable as Western philosophy compared to German [philosophy]."[54]

Cohen's fantasy of a German-Jewish *Wahlverwandtschaft*, Rosenzweig observed, served to exemplify the paradox of the cultured German Jew.[55] In contrast to other educated individuals, who are bound by powerful primordial bonds to the uneducated classes of their respective countries and who are thus to that extent estranged from other educated Europeans, the Jews alone consistently maintain a fidelity to European culture. This paradox allows Cohen to juxtapose that which has indeed remained separate: his abiding Jewish sensibility and his Deutschtum or, rather, his engagement with European culture.

Rosenzweig thus deems Cohen's philosophical idealizations to be a caricature of the social reality of German Jewry. But as a "caricature,"[56] it has the decisive value of highlighting "in gigantically magnified terms" what otherwise was but a vague, albeit pervasive, assumption.[57] Through Cohen's bold and eloquent incantations of a sacred partnership between Judentum and Deutschtum, the "and" of the German-Jewish reality was willy-nilly projected in its differentiating capacity and firmly lodged in the consciousness of the German Jew. By elevating the relationship of Germans and Jews to that of a partnership based on parity and borne of a "spiritual affinity," Cohen necessarily underscored the "and" of the equation to emphasize its function in demarcating a boundary and differentiating identities. Rosenzweig noted further that in urging German Jews to take both components of their identity as Germans and Jews with utmost earnestness, Cohen buttressed the "and" as a demarcation between two distinct realities. As Rosenzweig comments, "the 'and' is only a problem if both *Deutschtum* and *Judentum* are taken seriously."[58] Cohen left to the succeeding generation, Rosenzweig's generation, the task of guarding the integrity of this "and" and clarifying the nature of the relation between Judentum and Deutschtum.

As Rosenzweig envisioned it, the recrystallization of this relation would, in the first instance, require German Jewry's reaffirmation of itself as both a people and a spiritual vocation. Unlike many other Liberal Jews, Cohen also acknowledged the Jews to be a nation, but a nation only in the sense, as he put it, of an anthropological "means" to bear witness to the idea of Judaism.[59] In Rosenzweig's judgment, Cohen had erred, for it is misleading to conceive of Judaism simply as the religion of the Jews, and of the Jews merely as custodians of the sublime vision of ethical monotheism. Judaism is, Rosenzweig contended, intimately bound to the life of the Jewish people.[60] Accordingly, a genuine Jewish theology must include the Jewish family and community among its primary data.

Rosenzweig credited Martin Buber with fulfilling a crucial role in quickening a new appreciation of the life of the Jewish people as the matrix of the religious imagination and sensibility of Israel. Through hasidic tales and anecdotes published in the decade before the First World War, the young Buber acquainted educated Germans and Jews alike with the folk wisdom and native religiosity of pre-Emancipation Jewry. Rosenzweig, however, was wary of the young Buber's romantic enthusiasm and tendency to obscure God's revelatory transcendence by identifying Jewish folk religiosity with the then fashionable pantheistic mysticism.[61] Appropriately, after a debate between the anti-Zionist Cohen, for whom Israel, the Jewish people, were the guardian of the idea of God's transcendent Oneness, and the Zionist Buber, who celebrated Israel as a living, national reality, Rosenzweig commented that Buber and Cohen each heard only one part of the *shema*, the

ancient prayer summoning Israel into existence (see Deu-
teronomy 6:4). Buber seems to respond just to the first
part, "Hear, O Israel," whereas Cohen emphasizes the second, "God is One."[62] The Jewish spiritual reality, however,
is grounded in both components of the shema: the Jewish people, the living people of Israel, are summoned to
affirm the unity of the living, transcendent God. Again,
Rosenzweig regarded it as the dialectical destiny of his
generation to weld together anew the two components of
the shema, allowing it to regain its primal fullness in the
life of the Jewish people.

Rosenzweig appealed to the Jews to overcome their liberal scruples and reassert themselves as a people of a special order, as a people devoted to a divine covenant. Liberal
Judaism of the nineteenth century, he acknowledged, implicitly accepted this proposition by promoting the notion
of Israel's "universal mission."[63] Divorced from the traditional presupposition that Israel was a living community
bound by a unique, divinely ordained destiny, the notion
of a mission was designed largely to engender a sense of
Israel's abiding relevance in a liberal age. This relevance
was invariably defined in terms of concepts derived from
the regnant philosophical idiom. Cohen, for instance, defined Israel's vocation in the light of the ethical idealism
espoused by the Kantians. Cohen, Rosenzweig asserted,
hence fell into the "apologetic" trap of judging Judaism according to the criteria of world culture.

Cohen, like his nineteenth-century predecessors, therefore places Judaism within the realm of culture. But Judaism, Rosenzweig avowed, is not essentially a culture—
although, to be sure, it abounds in cultural expressions. In
contrast to a culture, Judaism has an essential wisdom that
is not refracted through acts of the human imagination,
which, by definition, unfold in history. (In passing, we may

note the Hegelian inflections of Rosenzweig's conception of culture.) Though embodied in the life of a people, Judaism attests to revealed, metahistorical and hence metacultural truths.[64]

As Rosenzweig tersely put it, "The Jews did not create their God but received and gave witness to him."[65] Israel was born—and is sustained—apart from culture. Yet from their very beginnings the Jews have eagerly partaken in the culture of others. Indeed, as Rosenzweig observed, "the impulse to assimilate . . . is as old as the people itself."[66] The formative myths of the Jews point to their consciousness as a people living among others and rejecting self-enclosed autonomy. But assimilation to a culture of others did not mean spiritual absorption. It was the lot of the Jews to remain strangers, "alien to all spiritual possessions of the nations, alien at heart even to the share we [Jews] ourselves try to contribute and recompense."[67]

According to Rosenzweig's reading of the spiritual biography of German Jewry, then, Jews have a dual destiny: to live simultaneously within and beyond culture, within and beyond time. "For all other peoples . . . know the world *(die Welt)* only as *eine Umwelt*," as an environment, a world circumscribed by place and time. "To us alone the *Umwelt* may never represent the world; the moment that the world breathes can never fully represent the future. The trials and tribulations of the day are to be found in the *Umwelt*—the fortress of the other peoples and even of our own community—but the ultimate meaning of our existence as a people constantly pushes us beyond the *Umwelt*."[68] These remarks are in consonance with Rosenzweig's view that the Jews, when adhering to their calling as a community of prayer and study, are a uniquely metahistorical community.[69]

Both the sociological and spiritual configurations of

Jewish life place the Jews beyond history and the struggle to master the here and now, beyond the Sisyphean efforts to control the Umwelt through the ploys of politics and secular wizardry. As a people of Exile, the Jews know the folly of political power; and as a people whose experience of time is determined by the sacred rhythms of their liturgical calendar, the Jews proleptically experience the eschatological future in which creation and history are reconciled in eternal peace. The Jewish people thus prefigure an absolute, redeemed reality beyond the conceits and anguish of history.[70]

Because Judaism is ensconced in an absolute reality, it cannot be properly compared, much less harmonized, with any historical reality or culture. Yet by virtue of its special relation to the Christian church, wedded to history through its affiliation with the gentile nations, Israel has the providential role of prodding the "peoples of the world" to push history beyond itself to the absolute future, the eschaton.[71]

Nestled in metahistorical seclusion, Judaism stands in a critical tension with history and culture. Individual Jews, however, live this tension within themselves, for they are both denizens of the metahistorical reality of Judaism and participating citizens of the Umwelt. As noted, the requickening of this primal tension of the Jewish soul—repressed in the age of the Ghetto—was the dialectical task that Rosenzweig assigned to German Jewry.

The revitalization of this tension was focused on the emergence of that elusive "and" linking the bifurcated soul of the German Jew. Rosenzweig resolutely contended that the desired revitalization would only be fully attained when the Jews took Judaism as seriously as their new love, Deutschtum. Nurtured to maturity, the "and" is not the separative "and" of Mendelssohn and his epigoni; nor is it

the harmonizing "and" of Hermann Cohen and his liberal
followers; rather, it is an emphatic "and" denoting a tension—Rosenzweig would undoubtedly say a creative tension—one necessary for the survival of Judaism as a spiritually vital and engaging form of existence.

But this "and," Rosenzweig cautioned, cannot simply
be evoked; it cannot be cajoled into existence by sermonic
appeals to primordial sentiment and loyalty. This "and"—
this tension—can be attained only if Judaism is a "living
reality," at least equal in its power to Deutschtum. Since
the Jews' heady flight from the ghetto to the bosom of German Kultur, Judaism had been steadily drained of its vitality, both existentially and intellectually. The challenge
faced by Rosenzweig's generation, as he conceived of it,
was to restore this vitality without severing the Jews' in-
volvement in Deutschtum and world culture. He was convinced that the spiritual renewal of Judaism did not have
to entail a diminished devotion to German culture. "I am
perhaps innocent," he wrote to a friend, "with respect to
the problem of *Deutschtum* and *Judentum.* I believe my
return to Judaism *(Verjudung)* has not made me a worse
but a better German. I do not in any way view the generation before us as better Germans."[72] He continued, "Were
someone to suspend me on tenterhooks, tearing me into
two pieces, I would surely know with which of these two
halves my heart . . . would go; I also know that I would not
survive the operation."[73] It is worth noting that one of the
very last projects that Rosenzweig undertook during his
tragically short life was a translation into German of the
biblical book of Isaiah, undertaken with Martin Buber, and
a newspaper series reviewing phonographic recordings of
German classical music from Bach to Bruckner.

Rosenzweig's affirmation of the "and" was not only
prompted by the practical need to accommodate the irre-

fragable fact that he was both a Jew and a cultured German, a person bound to the Torah and beholden to world culture. It was also inspired by theological considerations. The Jew, after all, is enjoined to sanctify creation—which, as Rosenzweig taught, is not only the domain of nature but also the realm of culture. Rosenzweig would speak of the "star of redemption"—the divine truth instantiated by Judaism—which is constituted by God's revelation, the terminus a quo of the cosmic drama, which reaches its destination, redemption, by traversing and hallowing creation.

To assume their pristine role in this drama, Rosenzweig said, the Jews must first repossess Judaism from within. They cannot proceed, however, the way they would in acquiring other forms of knowledge, that is, by simply adding Jewish knowledge to their culture. The German "may possess another civilization—ancient or modern—because and insofar as it belongs to the spiritual world that includes him; therefore he can acquire it without leaving his own world, maybe even without understanding its language, because in any event he will understand it only as translated into the 'language' of his world."[74] Nor is Judaism to be reclaimed as a civil religion—"for we are not concerned with creating an emotional center," informed by Jewish symbols and concepts, in support of the social and cultural values of the contemporary world.[75] The "Jewish sphere," Rosenzweig boldly exclaimed, is "independent from, even opposed to, [one's] non-Jewish surroundings."[76] There is a fundamental incommensurability between Judaism and world culture that can be bridged neither by translation nor by interpretation. The decisive difference between the Jewish world and that of Deutschtum is, then, not hermeneutical but ontological. And as a distinctive ontological reality, the Jewish world can ultimately be appropriated only existentially.[77]

Rosenzweig did not wish to imply that knowledge of Judaism is irrelevant. What was crucial was that the endeavor to know Judaism not be guided by an overriding search for a tertium quid, a comparative grid with which to catalogue the wisdom of Israel and place it in the syncretistic library of the cultured. Judaism must be encountered as an autonomous reality, primed by its distinctive cognitive and existential power. In the light of the imperious presence of Deutschtum—flush with bias against the spirit of Israel—Judaism was overshadowed and banished to some parochial corner where it ceased to be a commanding power in the life of most German Jews. Since Moses Mendelssohn most Jews have not, in fact, faced an "and" but an insidious "or," observed Rosenzweig—the exciting new world of imagination and the spirit opened by Deutschtum "or" the seemingly anachronistic and increasingly inaccessible world of Judaism. This insidious "or" must be replaced by an "and." The relation of Judentum and Deutschtum must cease to be that of a choice—an "or." It must be a relation founded in an authentically compelling "and." But in the absence of a genuine "and," the choice—the "or"—presented to the modern Jew is, of course, no real choice at all. The Jew qua Jew is truly free only by virtue of an "and," that is, when he or she is firmly centered in Judentum as well as in Deutschtum.

It was precisely the re-centering of the Jew in Judaism that Rosenzweig discerned to be the supreme task of the Jewish Renaissance, which reached full flower in the years of the Weimar Republic. And it was Rosenzweig's genius— which undoubtedly was in part the source of his great appeal to his contemporaries—to have realized that the way back from the "periphery" of acculturation and assimilation to the center of Jewish life could not be effected by a magical lobotomization of all that Jews acquired at the periphery.[78] The process of re-centering the Jew could be sustained only by laboriously and delicately reconstructing Jewish knowledge and faith while fully maintaining a respect for the intellectual sensibilities and cultural reflexes that have come to define the German Jew (and, if I may extrapolate, all modern Jews).

The Free Jewish House of Study (Freies Jüdisches Lehrhaus), which Rosenzweig founded in Frankfurt in 1920 and which was dedicated to an earnest study of Judaism free of all doctrinal fetters and arbitrary judgments, implicitly recognized the legitimacy of the "and"[79]—implicitly, because the "and," Rosenzweig explained, was to be neither proclaimed nor consciously cultivated. The "and" was to be fostered simply by tacitly respecting the culture of the participants at Rosenzweig's house of study while giving them the opportunity to "know Judaism as Judaism," to encounter Judaism as a living reality. This "and" was the presupposition of the Jewish Renaissance, but Rosenzweig provided no prescription or general formula for living with the "and." The re-centering of the Jew in Judaism would merely grant each individual the freedom to choose his or her "way of living with the 'and.'"

Once established as a genuine, existential reality, the "and" will perforce lead to the reintegration of Judaism— or, rather, the Jewish point of view—into general culture. "What we receive," wrote Rosenzweig, "we must receive as Jews, and yet in order to guarantee our integrity [*Einheit der Seele*], we must put our Jewishness in some kind of relation to what we give and to what we receive."[80] With a critical eye on the apologetic gyrations of nineteenth-century Jewish thought, he quickly appended a caveat: "We are the sole judges of any effort to grasp the world in Jewish terms."[81] Jewish theology was thus not a self-conscious exercise in philosophizing about Judaism but preeminently a mode of thinking about the world from *within* the experience of Judaism. The Jewish point of view, Rosenzweig held, can bear decisively on the larger issues of humanity and the quest to understand the meaning and purpose of creaturely existence. The reintegration of Judaism into the discourse of thinking humanity was, he believed, the ultimate and greatest achievement of German Jewry.

Thus Rosenzweig concluded his "eulogy" for German Jewry. To be sure, he spoke from the perspective of the penultimate chapter of German-Jewish history. Soon after his death, the forces of destruction rushed in to obliterate whatever hope there was for a sustained spiritual renewal of Judaism in Germany. Indeed, without the inclusion of the Holocaust in its purview, any eulogy for German Jewry is incomplete. But eulogies are incomplete by their very nature. Addressed to those who have survived the deceased, eulogies are meant to comfort, edify, and remind the survivors that they are the heirs of the departed, that they are charged by fate to complete or at least carry on the "good works" and tasks of the one whom they commemorate. In that all modern Jews are to a great measure the heirs of German Jewry, they are beckoned by the sacred memory of this ill-fated community to learn to live honorably with the "and" that characterizes their parallel reality as Jews and as citizens of a world culture. Rosenzweig was alert to the perils attendant on a life of divided passions, but, as he declared, it is "eine geliebte Gefährdung," a danger we embrace with love, "a danger we would not wish to miss."[82]

Epilogue
Reflections on the Legacy of German Jewry

A postcard written by Franz Kafka in 1916 provides a sardonic gloss on the problematic discussed in this volume. Having just read two radically divergent reviews of his work—one finding in it something quintessentially German,[1] the other regarding it as the representative "Jewish document of our time"[2]—he dashed off a note to a friend, asking, "Am I a circus acrobat riding astride two horses? Sadly I am not. Rather I lie flat on my back!"[3] With a humorous twist, Kafka exposes the difficulty of endeavoring to live with a Jewish and a German, or European, cultural identity.

Though compelling, Kafka's image of a daring balancing act may ultimately be misleading. Certainly Rosenzweig, applauding a vision of a New Babylon, would have argued that it is misleading. Evoking the memory of ancient Babylon—where, at the convergence of two mighty rivers and several civilizations, Judaism attained new creative impulses and crystallized as a religious culture—Rosenzweig averred that the attempt to dwell in multiple cultures and spiritual universes need not lead to the humiliating absurdity intimated by Kafka. The German Jew, he affirmed, nurtured by two distinct spiritual sources —Judaism and European culture—could become paradigmatic for all modern Jews, indeed, by implication, for all

individuals who lay claim to various, often radically contrasting spiritual and cultural estates. What is crucial, in
his judgment, as we saw in the previous chapter, is that
the "and" conjoining those estates preserve the cognitive
integrity of each while allowing for a free and genuine
dialogue between them. So conceived, the "and" is not
a hyphen fusing different cultural identities but a bridge
granting easy, untroubled access to each of these distinct,
forever-separate realms of the human spirit.

Learning to be a German—or, more accurately, a par-
ticipant in European humanistic culture—*and* a Jew,
Rosenzweig reasoned, was the challenge inherently posed
by the Enlightenment and Emancipation. Feeling that German Jewry had in his generation attained the spiritual and
intellectual maturity to meet the challenge, he spoke of a
Jewish Renaissance and envisioned a New Babylon arising
on German soil.[4] This vision takes on a tragically ironic
dimension when one notes that Hitler came to power just
over three years after Rosenzweig's death in December
1929.

The vision thus may be seen as an example of the naïveté that allegedly benighted German Jewry. Bearing an
obsessive desire to be accepted by a nation that recurrently
debated their eligibility for full-fledged citizenship, German Jews are said to have myopically overlooked the fact
that most Germans, even liberals and progressives, continued to regard them as outsiders, as alien interlopers.
As I have argued throughout this essay, particularly in the
first two chapters, the German-Jewish intellectual elite
was hardly innocent about antisemitism. This was also
true during the years of the Weimar Republic, when Rosenzweig proposed his vision of a New Babylon. Although the
new order established by the liberal constitution of the republic allowed former outsiders to become insiders (to em-

ploy once again Peter Gay's apt image),[5] it soon became evident to many that the Jews would remain outsiders in the eyes of most Germans.[6] Hence, the appointment of Walther Rathenau (1867–1922) as foreign minister of the fledgling republic was greeted by German Jewry not with jubilation but with trepidation. Shortly after Rathenau took office, he was visited by Albert Einstein and Kurt Blumenfeld, the leader of the Zionist movement in Germany, who appealed to him to resign. They are reported to have told him that at this juncture in German history "a Jew could at most be the Minister of Posts, not Foreign Minister."[7] Several months later, Rathenau was assassinated by right-wing opponents of the Weimar constitution, who contemptuously labeled the new state a "Judenrepublik."

To be sure, the leadership of the Jewish community kept up a brave front,[8] intoning the oft-repeated refrain "Na also, es geht ja immer besser und besser."[9] But beneath the facade were inchoate feelings that all was not well, that the situation was tenuous both for the republic and for German Jewry. It would be mistaken, however, to conclude that a studied optimism distorted the vision of German Jews, blinding them to the dangers lurking in the dark—dangers they allegedly perceived but chose to ignore or play down. Gershom Scholem implies this in his condemnation of what he regards as the delusive fantasy of a German-Jewish dialogue or symbiosis; he suggests that in promoting a myth of harmonious relations with cultured non-Jewish Germans, German Jews undercut their resolve to confront the harsh realities facing them.[10]

Scholem and those who advance similar arguments are to be faulted on methodological and substantive grounds. The indictment of pre-Holocaust generations of German Jews for courting peril by endorsing the myth of a German-Jewish symbiosis is burdened by the fallacy of retrospec-

tive judgment. Viewed in the light of the horrid events
ushered in by the Nazis' assumption of power in January 1933, the dangers—which German Jewry undeniably
on the whole refused to confront—indeed take on catastrophic dimensions; but considered from the perspective
of Auschwitz, those dangers assume a magnitude that
those contemporary with the Weimar Republic could not
possibly have foreseen, even by individuals who were
alert to the many social and political contradictions that
plagued the ill-fated state. As Jacob Katz has argued, although it may be possible for historians to explain by the
wisdom of hindsight the logical sequence of events leading
to the advent of the Third Reich and the crazed schemes
it was to institute, it is epistemologically erroneous to assume that contemporaries could—not to say, should—have
had the same knowledge that historians have at their dis-
posal.[11] That knowledge is ex post facto by definition. As
Katz reminds us, in assessing the judgments and actions of
individuals in a particular historical context, historians are
obliged to bracket their knowledge of subsequent developments, for that knowledge was not available to the individuals under scrutiny. Katz appropriately cites the Dutch
historian Johan Huizinga, who said, "The past must be
imagined as if it were still the present"[12]—that is, without
introducing a knowledge of future developments. Adhering
to this principle, one cannot assume that the Holocaust,
with all its horrific dimensions, could have been foreseen.
Vaticination *ex eventu* is a theological device not recommended to historians or sympathetic observers of the past.

    More pertinent to the topic of his volume, however, is
the fact that the notion of a German-Jewish symbiosis is
preeminently a post–Second World War construct largely
propounded by non-Jews expressing an idealized image of a
world brutally disrupted by Hitler. When German Jews like

Hermann Cohen, however, spoke of the affinity between Deutschtum and Judentum, they were not speaking principally of such an imagined symbiosis, of a cultural dialogue between Germans and Jews, but rather of an inner Jewish dialogue—of a dialogue within the soul of individual Jews as well as between themselves. They knew they had few non-Jewish partners in the dialogue.[13] They saw the problem as how to preserve Jewish cultural memory and identity while passionately and creatively embracing another culture.

Here it would be apposite to reiterate Gustav Landauer's statement, cited as the epigraph to this volume and discussed in Chapter 2: "I have never had the need to simplify myself or to create an artificial unity through denial; I accept my complexity and hope to be even more many-sided than I am now aware of."[14] Though proud of and comfortable with his Jewish identity,[15] Landauer proclaimed that he was no longer just a Jew: having access to many cultures, he had multiple cultural identities.[16] His thematization of the issue was, as I noted, picked up by his friend Buber, who concurred that modern Jews are an "admixture" of many cultures.[17]

The true challenge, Buber insisted, is not to simplify oneself but to master the admixture so that one's primordial Jewish cultural identity is not lost in a syncretistic brew. Though a man of universal culture, Buber found the syncretism endorsed by many cosmopolitans, such as Landauer, to be unsatisfactory. Once absorbed into European culture—with its claims to being a high culture and thus a superseding, if not explicitly a superior, culture—Judaism was bound to lose its integrity as a distinctive culture engaging the intellectual passion and imagination of Jews. For Buber, as for Rosenzweig and, indeed, for all the advocates of a German-Jewish Renaissance,[18] the issue was how to participate in a variety of cultures without privileging any—either the European or the Jewish.

Rosenzweig's vision of a New Babylon was thus an attempt to establish a symmetry or, to employ Kafka's image, a balance between Jewish and other cultural identities. This vision also represented a criticism of those who advocated Jewish renewal—the rescuing of Judaism from the corrosive swirl of modern culture with its secular and assimilatory impulses—by denying one's "non-Jewish" identities and affiliations. The revitalization of Judaism did not require (as Landauer and Benjamin had feared), the spiritual and cultural reghettoization of the Jew. The vision of a New Babylon—whether it was to be realized in Germany or, according to Buber and other cultural Zionists, under the aegis of a new Jewish spiritual center in the land of Israel—was an acknowledgment that the modern Jew is irrefragably bifurcated, that two souls dwell in his breast.

This was the undeniable reality of German Jewry. The German-Jewish symbiosis was *within* the mind of the Jew, regardless of whether or not it existed *between* the Jew and non-Jewish German. This observation allows us to understand how German Jews could remain true to German culture under the Third Reich. Indeed, their response to National Socialism was precisely to reassert their attachment to German culture, that is, the German humanistic tradition. Upon Hitler's seizure of power, the Jews were systematically removed from public and cultural life. To accommodate Jewish artists and performers, now permitted to appear only before purely Jewish audiences, the Jüdische Kulturbund was established.[19] The repertoire of the Kulturbund—which embraced the full gamut of the arts, from theater and opera to symphonic and chamber music—included at its center the works of the greatest playwrights and composers of Germany. This affirmation of German culture was not only a grand act of defiance but also a reflection of German Jewry's deepest inner reality.

At the height of the Holocaust, the Bulgarian-born, German-language author Elias Canetti gave expression to this sensibility, which has come to define German Jewry for all those who honor its legacy: "Should I harden myself against the Russians because there are Jews, against the Chinese because they are far away, against the Germans because they are possessed by the devil? Can't I still belong to all of them, as before, and nevertheless be a Jew?"[20]

Notes

Chapter One. The Bifurcated Soul of the German Jew

1. Heinrich Heine, *A Journey from Munich to Genoa*, chap. 7, cited in S. S. Prawer, *Heine's Jewish Comedy: A Study of His Portraits of Jews and Judaism* (Oxford: Oxford University Press, Clarendon Press, 1983), epigraph on title page.

2. This incomplete picturesque novella is appended to Heine's volume of poems *Der Salon: Erster Band* (Hamburg: Hoffmann und Campe, 1834). All translations from the German are mine unless otherwise specified.

3. I wish to thank Phillip Sievert Blom, formerly of Merton College, Oxford, for bringing this passage in Heine's novella to my attention.

4. Translated in Prawer, *Heine's Jewish Comedy*, p. 242.

5. Though not identical, the terms *Bildung* and German (enlightened) *Kultur* historically overlap. See Franz Rauhut, "Die Herkunft der Worte und Begriffe: 'Kultur,' 'Civilization,' und 'Bildung,'" *Germanisch-Romanische Monatsschrift* 111 (1953): 89–91.

6. This critique of the notion of a German-Jewish symbiosis is most prominently and eloquently represented by Gershom Scholem. See his essays "Against the Myth of the German-Jewish Dialogue," "Once More: The German-Jewish Dialogue," and "Jews and Germans," in his *On Jews and Judaism in Crisis: Selected Essays*, ed. Werner J. Dannhauser (New York: Schocken Books, 1976), pp. 61–92. For a judicious selection of the major texts in the "symbiosis debate" and for an illuminating introduction, see Christoph Schulte, ed., *Deutschtum und Judentum: Ein Disput unter Juden aus*

Deutschland (Stuttgart: Philipp Reclam jun., 1993). In the Epilogue I consider what I deem to be the logical fallacies inherent in the charge that German Jewry's naïveté regarding the symbiosis led them to ignore the "catastrophic" potential of antisemitism.

7. Hence, for example, the American Historical Association, convening for an annual meeting in San Francisco in December 1973, hosted a symposium entitled "German Jews: From Assimilation to Auschwitz." Notice in *Leo Baeck Institute Year Book* 20 (1975): 3.

8. Benno Jacob, "Prinzipielle Bemerkungen zu einer zionistischen Schrift," *Der Morgen* 5 (1927): 527–531, cited in Jacob Katz, "German Culture and the Jews," in *The Jewish Response to German Culture: From the Enlightenment to the Second World War*, ed. Jehuda Reinharz and Walter Schatzberg (Hanover: University Press of New England, 1985), p. 86.

9. See David Sorkin, "Emancipation and Assimilation: Two Concepts and Their Application to German-Jewish History," *Leo Baeck Institute Year Book* 35 (1990): 17–33. Also see Jacob Katz, *Emancipation and Assimilation: Studies in Modern Jewish History* (Westmean: Gregg International Publishers, 1972); and Jacob Toury, "Emancipation and Assimilation: Concepts and Conditions" (Hebrew), in *Yalkut Moreshet* 2 (1954): 167–182.

10. Employing the concept "dissimilation," Shulamit Volkov discusses the dialectical forces that emerged from within the process of assimilation to draw "German Jews back together again [as Jews] even despite themselves." Volkov, "The Dynamics of Dissimilation: *Ostjuden* and German Jews," in *Jewish Response to German Culture*, ed. Reinharz and Schatzberg, pp. 195–211; the quotation is from p. 196. For a similar argument, framed in more theoretical terms, see the perspicacious essay by the late Amos Funkenstein, "Dialectics of Assimilation," *Jewish Social Studies* 1.2 (Winter 1995): 1–14. On the various identities of the modern Jew, particularly the German Jew, see Michael A. Meyer, *Jewish Identity in the Modern World* (Seattle: University of Washington Press, 1990).

11. Gerson D. Cohen, "German Jewry as a Mirror of Modernity," *Leo Baeck Institute Year Book* 20 (1975): xi.

12. See Lewis D. Wurgaft, "Identity in World History: A Postmodern Perspective," *History and Theory* 34 (1995): 67–85.

13. Louis Dumont, *German Ideology* (Chicago: University of Chicago Press, 1994), p. 3.

14. Ibid.

15. Ibid., p. 7.

16. Territory is meant here in a geopolitical sense. Since the early nineteenth century, German romantics have celebrated the German landscape, especially its forests, as the unique, defining patrimony of the German nation. See the detailed essays in the handsomely produced catalogue of an exhibit sponsored by the Berlin Akademie der Künste, *Waldungen: Die Deutschen und ihr Wald*, ed. Bernd Weyergraf (Berlin: Akademie der Künste, 1987).

17. See Bernard Giesen, *Die Intellektuellen und die Nation: Eine deutsche Achsenzeit* (Frankfurt: Suhrkamp, 1993), pp. 200-232. Also see Shmuel Noah Eisenstadt and Bernard Giesen, "The Construction of Collective Identity," *Archives européennes de sociologie* 36 (1995): 72-101.

18. On the political history leading to the formation of a unified German nation-state, see James J. Sheehan, *German History, 1770-1866* (New York: Oxford University Press, 1989).

19. Helmut Plessner, *Verspätete Nation: Über die politische Verführbarkeit des bürgerlichen Geistes*, 5th ed. (Frankfurt: Suhrkamp, 1994). In a critique of Plessner's thesis, Otto Dann argues that a *Reichsnationalismus* effectively displaced the *Volksnationalismus* and allowed Germany to mature as a nation-state. See Dann, *Nation und Nationalismus in Deutschland, 1770-1990* (Munich: C. H. Beck, 1993).

20. Plessner argues that even after the founding of the Second Reich, German collective identity remained bound to these alternative conceptions. Thus, he entitles his chapters dealing with the Second Reich "Bismarcks Reich, eine Großmacht ohne Staatsidee" (Bismarck's Reich, a great power without a concept of state) and "Nicht Staat, sondern Volk" (Not a state, but a people). Plessner, *Verspätete Nation*, pp. 43, 52. See "Civic codes have never been prevalent in the construction of German identity." Eisenstadt and Giesen, "Construction of Collective Identity," p. 93. Also see Rudolf von Thadden's comparative study of German and French national identities in the nineteenth century, which takes its point of departure from Jürgen Habermas's call for post–World War II Germans to break with the political past of Germany and

develop a "Verfassungspatriotismus" (constitutional patriotism)—that is, to construct a national identity on solely civic
or constitutional criteria. Rudolf von Thadden, "Aufbau natio-
naler Identität: Deutschland und Frankreich im Vergleich,"
in *Nationale und kulturelle Identität: Studien zur Entwick-
lung des kollektiven Bewußtseins in der Neuzeit*, ed. Bernard
Giesen (Frankfurt: Suhrkamp, 1991), pp. 493–512.

21. The term *Deutschtum* is used here somewhat anach-
ronistically. According to the 1860 edition of the Grimm
brothers' historical dictionary of the German language,
Deutschtum gained currency only "recently" and usually in-
volves an ironic reference to an exaggerated attachment to
reputed German values. Cf. "Deutschtum: N. [Nomen] für
Deutschheit ist erst in der letzten Zeit aufgekommen, doch
wird es meist ironisch gebraucht, man will damit übertrie-
bene Anhänglichkeit an deutsches Wesen bezeichnen." Jacob
and Wilhelm Grimm, *Deutsches Wörterbuch* (Leipzig, 1860),
11:1053.

22. Wolfgang Benz, "Die Legende von der deutsch-
jüdischen Symbiose," *Merkur: Deutsche Zeitschrift für euro-
päisches Denken* 45.2 (February 1991): 168.

23. The term *Bildungsbürgertum* is an analytical construct of historians of Central Europe; it appeared in the
1920s. See Ulrich Engelhardt, *"Bildungsbürgertum": Begriffs-
und Dogmengeschichte eines Etiketts* (Stuttgart: Klett-Cotta,
1986), p. 189. On the applicability of the term, despite its
ambiguities, see Jürgen Kocka, "The European Pattern and the
German Case," in *Bourgeois Society in Nineteenth-Century
Europe*, ed. Kocka and Allen Mitchell (Oxford: Berg, 1993),
pp. 23–24. Kocka argues that in Germany the term actually used by the middle classes, *Bürgertum*, did not have a
Marxian or Weberian connotation, for it included individuals who did not strictly belong to these conceptions of the
middle class; nor was the term equivalent to *burgher*, used
for the late medieval and early modern townspeople who constituted a specific *Stand*, or corporate group, enjoying legally
defined privileges. A "post-corporate supra-local social formation," the Bürgertum included individuals of economic and
professional attainment who shared both a self-conscious dis-
tance from the nobility and monarchy and a distinct set
of cultural values. Whereas a minimum level of economic

well-being was a necessary qualification for belonging to the German Bürgertum, it was thus not the sole or most significant criterion for membership. Accordingly, although the *Wirtschaftsbürgertum* (the economic middle class) and the Bildungsbürgertum overlapped, they were not identical. Of particular significance for the Jews, an "emphasis on education (rather than on religion) characterised [German] middle class views of themselves and the world. Simultaneously, education *(Bildung)* served as a basis on which they communicated with one another, and which distinguished them from others who did not share this type of (classical) education. There was much respect for scholarly pursuits *(Wissenschaft)* and a particular aesthetic appreciation of music, literature and the arts." Further, "bourgeois culture claimed universal recognition. In contrast to aristocratic or peasant cultures, it had an in-built tendency to expand beyond the social boundaries of the *Bürgertum* and to imprint the whole society. The *Verbürgerlichung* [bringing under the sway of middle-class values] of other social groups was an essential element of bourgeois culture." Ibid., pp. 6–7.

24. From the perspective of social history, Herbert A. Strauss questions the relevance of the term *Bildungsbürgertum,* commenting that its reference is "several rungs too high for the minuscule and diverse secular intelligentsia (almost invisible outside of Berlin and probably a few other places)." Strauss, "Emancipation History: Limits of Revisionism in the Post-Holocaust Period," *Leo Baeck Institute Year Book* 37 (1992): 106. This observation seems to ignore the considerations advanced by Kocka (see previous note) and other scholars with respect to the defining cultural attitudes of the German middle class, who as such embraced more than the attitudes formerly belonging to the intelligentsia or *Kulturträger* (the formal bearers and purveyors of culture); indeed, the term *Kulturträger* includes all those who engaged in the discourse and symbolic codes associated with the culture and ethos of Bildung. In the context of the Bildungsbürgertum, or the relatively broad social constituency supporting high culture, one may therefore speak of secondary Bildung. See the essays in *Bourgeois Society in Nineteenth-Century Europe,* the volume edited by Kocka and Mitchell cited in the previous note, which are drawn from the much larger work edited by

Kocka, *Bürgertum im 19. Jahrhundert: Deutschland im europäischen Vergleich*, 3 vols. (Munich: Deutscher Taschenbuch
Verlag, 1988). Also see Engelhardt, *"Bildungsbürgertum."*

25. The celerity and comprehensive nature of the Jews'
entry into the middle classes of Germany is highlighted by
their previous poverty: "at the end eighteenth century, it was
estimated that about 80 percent of the Jews living in Germany belonged to the lowest strata, 'living from hand to
mouth.'" Shulamit Volkov, "The 'Verbürgerlichung' of the
Jews as a Paradigm," in *Bourgeois Society*, ed. Kocka and
Mitchell, p. 368. Also see Jacob Toury, "Der Eintritt der Juden
ins deutsche Bürgertum," in *Das Judentum in der deutschen
Umwelt, 1800–1850: Studien zur Frühgeschichte der Emanzipation*, ed. Hans Liebeschütz and Arnold Paucker (Tübingen:
J. C. B. Mohr [Paul Siebeck], 1977), pp. 149–150; and Monika
Richarz, "Jewish Mobility in Germany During the Time of
Emancipation (1790–1871)," *Leo Baeck Institute Year Book* 20
(1975): 65–77.

26. Theodor Fontane, "An meinem Fünfundsiebzigsten,"
in his *Sämtliche Romane, Erzählungen, Gedichte, Nachgelas-
senes*, vol. 6 of *Werke, Schriften und Briefe*, 3d ed. (Munich:
Carl Hanser Verlag, 1995), p. 340f; the ellipsis after "the main
thing" is in the original. On the relationship between German writers and their Jewish readership, see Ernest K. Bramsted, *Aristocracy and the Middle Classes in Germany: Social
Types in German Literature, 1830–1900* (Chicago: University
of Chicago Press, 1964), pp. 262–268.

27. See Peter G. J. Pulzer, *The Rise of Political Anti-
Semitism in Germany and Austria* (New York: John Wiley and
Sons, 1964). On the Jewish responses to political and racial
antisemitism, see Ismar Schorsch, *Jewish Reactions to German Anti-Semitism, 1870–1914* (New York: Columbia University Press, 1972).

28. Jacob Katz, *Tradition and Crisis: Jewish Society at the
End of the Middle Ages* (New York: Free Press, 1961), chap. 23.

29. Cf. "The *Bildungsbürgertum*, the only social group
genuinely open to talent and potentially ready to accept Jews,
was from the outset ideologically so constituted that it could
in fact only partially welcome them." Volkov, "'Verbürgerlichung' of the Jews," p. 382.

30. Jacob Katz accordingly amended his earlier notion of a

"neutral society" (see note 27, above) to that of a "semi-neutral society." See his *Out of the Ghetto: The Social Background of Jewish Emancipation, 1770–1870* (Cambridge: Harvard University Press, 1973), chap. 4.

31. George Mosse, "Jewish Emancipation: Between *Bildung* and Respectability," in *Jewish Response to German Culture*, ed. Reinharz and Schatzberg, p. 10.

32. Aleida Assmann, *Arbeit am nationalen Gedächtnis: Eine kurze Geschichte der deutschen Bildungsidee* (Frankfurt: Campus Verlag, 1993).

33. The Jews were never totally alone. There were always sufficient numbers of non-Jewish Germans who subscribed to the same values as the liberal Jewish Bildungsbürgertum did to allow those Jews to believe they were part of a larger German project. See Dieter Langewiesche, ed., *Liberalismus im 19. Jahrhundert: Deutschland im europäischen Vergleich* (Göttingen: Vandenhoeck und Ruprecht, 1988); and Langewiesche, "Liberalism and the Middle Classes in Europe," in *Bourgeois Society*, ed. Kocka and Mitchell, pp. 40–69. On the image of liberalism in the nineteenth-century German novel, examined within the context of the struggle between the aristocracy and the bourgeoisie for social and political ascendancy, see Bramsted, *Aristocracy and the Middle-Classes in Germany*.

34. Implicit in Assmann's study is what she calls in her "Epilogue" *Erinnerungsarbeit*, "the work of memory" (*Arbeit am nationalen Gedächtnis*, p. 111), which she as a postwar German feels obliged to undertake in coming to terms with the awful heritage of National Socialism and the extermination of European Jewry. (This concern is also reflected in the very title of her book, translated as "Work on national memory.") As she also acknowledges in the conclusion of the volume, her study was thus guided by the question of why the idea of Bildung failed to promote a democratic political culture in Germany despite its initial liberal, cosmopolitan impulse. Identifying the root problem in the radical disjunction between culture and politics engendered by the ethic of Bildung, she notes that Bildung ultimately allowed Fascism and National Socialism to take hold in Germany. Cf. "The inner individualistic perfection through *Bildung* led Germany not to democracy but to monarchism and dictatorship. Nonethe-

less it is precisely the apolitical liberal idea of *Bildung* that [should be reclaimed], because it can serve as an ideological support for the new German democracy" (p. 106). Reaffirmed as a positive dimension of Germany's cultural memory, the ethic of Bildung—in its classical liberal image—could foster an axiological and epistemological humility that she deems necessary for a healthy democratic discourse. Here Assmann might have done well to quote Ernst Leopold Stahl's 1934 work on Bildung—which, written in the shadow of Hitler's diabolic regime (albeit published in neighboring Switzerland), takes on a defiant, heroic tone: "The idea of *Bildung* according to the philosophy of humanity requires that these capacities [of each individual assumed to be "original" and "unique"] be harmoniously developed and set forth in their particularity as well as in their totality. The important factor here is that particularity must be preserved, that there is no supreme law valid for all. There is, to be sure, something that is common, namely, the natural force present in all of us. But this assumes the most varied shapes and must also appear in its diversity." Stahl, *Die religiöse und humanitätsphilosophische Bildungsidee und die Entstehung des deutschen Bildungsromans im 18. Jahrhundert* (Bern, 1934), p. 24, cited in Dumont, *German Ideology*, p. 83.

35. Assmann, *Arbeit am nationalen Gedächtnis*, p. 24.

36. Hans Blumenberg, *Die Lesbarkeit der Welt* (Frankfurt: Suhrkamp, 1981), p. 177, cited in Assmann, *Arbeit am nationalen Gedächtnis*, p. 24f.

37. Assmann also notes that in calling for a transition from classical scholasticism to a Bildung grounded in a national language, namely, German, Herder in effect "nationalized" the concept of culture. "*Bildung* is for [Herder] the form of culture that binds itself with history. Herein it is distinguished from the learning of humanism as well as the Enlightenment." Assmann, *Arbeit am nationalen Gedächtnis*, p. 24.

38. Ibid., p. 25.

39. Ibid., pp. 40–66.

40. See note 36, above. Cf. "Under the influence of Humboldt's idea of the nation and as a result of the work of the brothers Grimm, local village dialects, for instance, gained a new dignity as the building blocks of a higher national language. An entire popular culture was accepted as complementary to bourgeois culture, considered outmoded perhaps,

but still part of the national heritage. . . . Yiddish, on the other hand, continued to be mercilessly derided [as uncultured]." Volkov, "The 'Verbürgerlichung' of the Jews as a Paradigm," p. 382. Also see Jacob Toury, "Die Sprache als Problem der jüdischen Einordnung im deutschen Kulturraum," *Jahrbuch des Instituts für deutsche Geschichte*, 4 (1982): 75–95.

41. Assmann, *Arbeit am nationalen Gedächtnis*, p. 35.

42. Ibid., p. 36.

43. Goethe, in his affirmative reply to Niethammer, suggested that the Jews serve as the model for Germany. The Jews, he reasoned, have endured through the millennia despite their lack of political power. The Germans would be wise were they to follow the Jews' example and seek to develop their own "national character" on the basis of, not political sovereignty *(Herrschaft)*, but culture. See ibid., p. 38 f.

44. Cf. Schiller's wistful query: "Deutschland? Aber wo liegt es? Ich weiß das Land nicht zu finden. Wo das Gelehrte beginnt, hört das Politische auf." (Germany? Where does one find her? I do not know how to find this country. Where [her] learning begins, [her] politics ends.) Schiller, *Sämtliche Werke* (Stuttgart, 1904), p. 103. See Bernhard Giesen and Kay Junge, "Vom Patriotismus zum Nationalismus: Zur Evolution der 'Deutschen Kulturnation,'" in *Nationale und kulturelle Identität*, ed. Giesen. pp. 255–303. The term "Kulturnation" was coined by Friedrich Meinecke, who introduced it in his *Weltbürgertum und Nationalstaat* (Munich, 1908). The concept existed *avant la lettre* as far back as the late Enlightenment. See Hans J. Hahn, *German Thought and Culture: From the Holy Roman Empire to the Present Day* (Manchester: Manchester University Press, 1995), pp. 92–99.

45. There were numerous partisan attempts to create a German national canon. Among the most notable was the 164-volume collection entitled *Deutsche National-Litteratur: Historisch-Kritische Ausgabe* (Berlin: Spemann Verlag, 1884–) initiated and edited by the writer Joseph Kürschner (1853–1902). Reaching back to works in old-high German and ultimately including writings of late nineteen-century authors, Kürschner sought with this ambitious project also to create a common German cultural memory. Shortly after Kürschner published the last volume of his "canon," Wilhelm Schwaner edited an anthology selected, as he put it, "from the holy scrip-

tures of the German peoples"; unhesitatingly he entitled the work *Die Germanenbibel* (Berlin, 1904). (I wish to thank Professor Gerold Frakes for bringing Kürschner's project to my attention.) See Walter Killy, "Zur Geschichte des deutschen Lesebuchs," in *Germanistik: Eine deutsche Wissenschaft*, ed. E. Lämmert et al. (Frankfurt: Suhrkamp, 1967), pp. 43–69; also see Peter Hohendahl, *Building a National Literature: The Case of German, 1830–1870*, trans. Renate Baron Franciscono (Ithaca: Cornell University Press, 1989); and Gregory Jusdanis, *Belated Modernity and Aesthetic Culture: Inventing National Literature* (Minneapolis: University of Minnesota Press, 1991).

46. Assmann, *Arbeit am nationalen Gedächtnis*, p. 66 f.

47. Wilhelm Dilthey, *Gesammelte Schriften* (Leipzig: Teubner Verlag, 1924), 5:9.

48. Assmann, *Arbeit am nationalen Gedächtnis*, p. 69.

49. Ibid., p. 70.

50. Ibid., p. 91. Assmann illustrates this contention by relating the following report from the Third Reich: Upon receiving orders to go to an assembly point for deportation, an eighty-year-old German Jewish woman committed suicide. Before taking the dosage of Veronal—which her grandson, a student of chemistry, had secured for her and upon whose witness the report is based—she bade farewell to the world by reciting verses from the German classics, especially the Thekla monologue in Schiller's trilogy, *Wallenstein*. Ibid.

51. Herbert Strauss rightly points out that German Jewry was far more economically and socially stratified than is suggested by associating it with the Bildungsbürgertum. This does not, however, gainsay the tendency of Jews since the early nineteenth century to gravitate to the urban centers and middle-class culture in disproportionate numbers and to conspicuously identify with the culture of Bildung, especially with what I have referred to as secondary Bildung (see note 23, above). See Strauss, "Emancipation History," p. 106.

52. The emergence of a ramified German-Jewish culture in the nineteenth century is discussed in Shulamit Volkov, *Die Erfindung einer Tradition: Zur Entstehung des modernen Judentums in Deutschland*, Schriften des Historischen Kollegs, Vorträge 29 (Munich: Stiftung Historisches Kolleg, 1998).

53. Auerbach's prolific and highly popular writings on German folklore, especially his programmatic *Schrift und*

Volk: Grundzüge der volksthümlichen Literatur . . . (1846), are analyzed in the context of his pronounced Jewish commitments in David Sorkin, "The Invisible Community: Emancipation, Secular Culture, and Jewish Identity in the Writings of Berthold Auerbach," in *Jewish Response to German Culture,* ed. Reinharz and Schatzberg, pp. 100–119, especially pp. 111–116. Auerbach's Jewish identity is discussed in Jacob Katz, "Berthold Auerbach's Anticipation of the German-Jewish Tragedy," *Hebrew Union College Annual* 53 (1982): 215–240; and Margarita Pazi, "Berthold Auerbach and Moritz Hartmann," *Leo Baeck Institute Year Book* 18 (1973): 201–218.

54. See Walter Laqueur, *Young Germany: A History of the German Youth Movement* (London: Routledge and Kegan Paul, 1962), pp. 155–166.

55. Toury, "Die Sprache als Problem der jüdischen Einordnung."

56. Alexander Altmann, "Moses Mendelssohn as the Archetypal German Jew," in *Jewish Response to German Culture,* ed. Reinharz and Schatzberg, p. 21.

57. Franz Rosenzweig, "Der jüdische Mensch (Entwurf für die erste Vorlesungsreihe im Freien Jüdischen Lehrhaus von Oktober bis Dezember 1920)," in Rosenzweig, *Zweistromland: Kleinere Schriften zu Glauben und Denken,* ed. Reinhold Mayer and Annemarie Mayer, section 3 of *Der Mensch und sein Werk: Gesammelte Schriften* (Dordrecht: Martinus Nijhoff, 1984), p. 566.

58. Also see my "Mendelssohn and Rosenzweig," *Journal of Jewish Studies* 38.2 (Autumn 1987): 203–211.

59. Moses Mendelssohn, *Jerusalem; or, On Religious Power and Judaism,* trans. Allan Arkush with an introduction and commentary by Alexander Altmann (Hanover: University Press of New England, 1983).

60. Wilhelm von Humboldt, "Über die Religion" (written in 1790 but first published in 1903); cited in Hans Liebeschütz, "Judentum und deutsche Umwelt im Zeitalter der Restauration," in *Das Judentum in der deutschen Umwelt,* ed. Liebeschütz and Paucker, p. 4.

61. See Nathan Rotenstreich, *Jews and German Philosophy: The Polemics of Emancipation* (New York: Schocken Books, 1984).

62. Johann Gottlieb Fichte, "Beitrag zur Berichtung der

Urteile des Publicums über die Französische Revolution"
(1793), in Fichte, *Sämtliche Werke* (Berlin, 1845), 6:150; cited
in P. Mendes-Flohr and J. Reinharz, *The Jew in the Modern
World: A Documentary History,* 2d rev. ed. (New York: Oxford
University Press, 1995), p. 309.

63. Ibid. See Jacob Katz, "A State Within a State: The
History of an Antisemitic Slogan," *Proceedings of the Israel
Academy of Sciences and Humanities* 4.3 (1969): 1–16, reprinted (in English) in Katz, *Zur Assimilation und Emanzipation der Juden: Ausgewählte Schriften* (Darmstadt: Wissen-
schaftliche Buchgesellschaft, 1982), pp. 124–153.

64. Writing in 1815, the Jewish publicist Saul Ascher recognized that Fichte's and others' contempt for the Jews and
Judaism served an integral nationalism that reflected, he
thought, an anxious but ever elusive quest for German unity:
"Christianity and Germanness were soon melted into one,
an easy task for transcendental idealists and identity philosophers. They reasoned this way: Germany could be saved only
by means of oneness and identity of the people in the Idea.
Oneness and identity in religion expresses this requirement
completely. . . . It ought not to seem strange that, according
to the ideas of these enthusiastic idealists . . . the antithesis to
their theory lay in the Jews, and this explains the coarse and
menacing tone in which, from Fichte at the end of the century [see note 61, above] to his students and admirers today,
the Jews and Jewry have been stormed at." Cited in Gordon
Craig, *The Germans* (New York: New American Library, 1983),
p. 131. The exclusion of the Jews from the "idea" of an integral
Germany can also be seen as indicative of the resistance to
cultural pluralism discussed in the following note.

65. Elsewhere I have suggested employing the concept of
"civil society"—whose criteria of membership also ultimately
determine the criteria of citizenship—as another means of
examining the same question. See Mendes-Flohr, "The Emancipation of European Jewry: Why Was It Not Self-Evident?"
Studia Rosenthaliana 30.1 (June 1996): 7–20 (this issue, which
contains the Proceedings of the Seventh International Symposium on the History and Culture of the Jews in the Netherlands, is entitled *Expectations and Confirmation: Two Hundred Years of Jewish Emancipation in the Netherlands* and
was edited by Commissie voor de Geschiedenis en de Cultuur

van de Joden in Nederland, Koninklijke Nederlandse Akademie van Wetenschappen). Jürgen Kocka insightfully points
out that the German term for "civil society" *(bürgerliche Gesellschaft)* contains a "semantic ambiguity" of far-reaching
importance: "*Bürger* means bourgeois and civil at the same
time," with "civil" denoting the social and legal framework
embracing individuals who are, at least *in potentia,* "citizens"
of a constitutional state. Kocka, "European Pattern and the
German Case," p. 9. If I may extrapolate, Jews would read the
term "civil society" as a signal that if only they became *Bürger,*
that is, bourgeoisie, would they ipso facto enjoy the status of
citizens. The Jews of Germany indeed became bourgeois before they became *Bürger,* that is, citizens. Alas, the transition
was not self-evident. Jewish emancipation was a protracted
process in which the eligibility of the Jews for citizenship and
political equality was, despite their economic and educational
attainments, hotly debated by liberals and conservatives alike.
Nor did the eventual achievement of political emancipation
and citizenship necessarily confer upon the Jews the dignity
of being regarded by non-Jewish citizens as fellow Germans.

66. "Mismeeting" *(Vergegnung)* is a term coined by Martin
Buber to designate an intended dialogue or a meeting between
an "I and Thou" that fails, usually because of misperceptions
or asymmetries in the situation. See Buber, "Autobiographical
Fragments," in *The Philosophy of Martin Buber,* ed. Paul A.
Schilpp and M. Friedman (London: Cambridge University
Press, 1967), p. 4.

67. On "horizons of expectations" *(Erwartungshorizonte),*
see Reinhart Koselleck, *Futures Past: On the Semantics of
Historical Time,* trans. Keith Tribe (Cambridge: MIT Press,
1985), pp. 267–289.

68. In this context, one should recall that in the trea-
tise *Jerusalem,* Mendelssohn grounded his defense of his dual
position as an observant Jew and an adherent of the Enlightenment in a systematic elaboration of a liberal conception of a
contractual or constitutional state. His arguments in support
of separation of religion and state, the inviolability of personal liberties, and the limitations of political power may be
viewed as anticipating the political theories of Thomas Jefferson. See Altmann's commentary in Mendelssohn, *Jerusalem,*
pp. 161, 240.

69. Influenced by Herder, Fichte, and the romantics, the conception of Germany as a *Volksnation* crystallized during the Napoleonic Wars, when the various German states and principalities sought to liberate themselves from French rule. See Dann, *Nation und Nationalismus in Deutschland*, p. 54 f.

70. Brian C. J. Singer, "Cultural Versus Contractual Nations: Rethinking Their Opposition." *History and Theory* 35.3 (1996): 311. Also see Roger Brubaker, *Citizenship and Nationhood in France and Germany* (Cambridge: Harvard University Press, 1992); and Dumont, *German Ideology*.

71. These typologies are further elaborated in Brubaker, *Citizenship and Nationhood in France and Germany*; Dumont, *German Ideology*; and Hans Kohn, *The Mind of Germany: The Education of a Nation* (London: Macmillan, 1960).

72. This is precisely the point of Singer's article mentioned in note 70, above.

73. In a comparative anthropological analysis of the modern ethos as manifest in France and Germany, Dumont develops what may be called a political anthropology of collective identities. See Dumont, *German Ideology*.

74. Mosse, "Jewish Emancipation: Between *Bildung* and Respectability," p. 14.

75. Cf., for example, Jakob and Wilhelm Grimm, eds., *Deutsche Sagen*, 3d ed. (Berlin: Nicolaische Verlagsbuchhandlung, 1892), 2:105, 208. For a succinct survey of the fashioning of the Barbarossa myth and its role in the construction of a German national identity, see Hahn, *German Thought and Culture*, pp. 13–26. Hahn reminds us that the Grimm brothers, like Herder and Fichte, were essentially liberals who affirmed the Enlightenment ideal of a universal humanity. Herder, for instance, held that the ideal would be best served by a "palingenesis," a rebirth into the natural state of humankind. On the narrowing of the concept of Volk by later generations of German thinkers and ideologues, see K. Minogue, *Nationalism* (Baltimore: John Hopkins University Press, 1973); and M. R. Lepius, "Nation und Nationalismus in Deutschland," in *Nationalismus in der Welt von heute*, ed. Heinrich A. Winkler (Göttingen: Vandenhoeck und Ruprecht, 1986).

76. Heinrich von Treitschke, "Unsere Aussichten" (1879), in *Der Berliner Antisemitismusstreit*, ed. Walter Boehlich (Frankfurt: Insel Verlag, 1965), p. 13. Heine made a similar ob-

servation regarding the Jews' cosmopolitan proclivities, but his evaluation was decidedly positive: "Europe is raising itself up to the Jews. I say 'raising itself up,' for from the very beginning the Jews bore within themselves the modern principle, which is only today becoming palpably manifest among the peoples of Europe. . . . The Jews adhered only to the law, the abstract idea, like our more recent cosmopolitan republicans, who respect as their highest good not the land of their birth or the person of their prince, but only the law. Cosmopolitanism, it might truly be said, sprang from the soil of Judea; and Christ who . . . was truly a Jew, had actually established a propaganda of world citizenship *(eine Propaganda des Weltbürgertums)."* Heine, "Shakespeares Mädchen und Frauen," in Heine, *Confessio Judaica: Eine Auswahl aus seinen Dichtungen, Schriften und Briefe,* ed. Hugo Bieber (Berlin: Welt Verlag, 1925), p. 124.

77. Ibid., p. 9 (emphasis added).

78. Heinrich von Treitschke, *History of Germany in the Nineteenth Century,* ed. Gordon Craig (Chicago: University of Chicago Press, 1975), 4:556.

79. Cf. "What we demand of our Israelite fellow citizens is simple: They should be Germans, feel themselves fully *(schlicht und recht)* German, without prejudice to their faith and ancient sacred memories, which we all respect; but what we do not want is that the thousand-year German civilization [*Gesittung;* the term also means "breeding" and "mores"] be displaced by an era of a German-Jewish hybrid culture *(Mischkultur)."* Ibid., p. 10. He later argued that whatever Judaism had to contribute to German culture had already been transmitted through Christianity. See Heinrich von Treitschke, "Noch einige Bemerkungen zur Judenfrage" (1880), in *Der Berliner Antisemitismusstreit,* ed. Boehlich, p. 85.

80. Treitschke, "Unsere Aussichten," p. 13.

81. Hans Leibeschütz, "Treitschke and Momsen on Jewry and Judaism," *Leo Baeck Institute Year Book* 7 (1962): 170–175; and Robert Weltsch, introduction to *Leo Baeck Institute Year Book* 7 (1962): xxvii.

82. Heinrich von Treitschke, "Herr Graetz und sein Judenthum" (1879), in *Der Berliner Antisemitismusstreit,* ed. Boehlich, p. 32. Graetz, in effect, demands "recognition of Judaism as a nation in and beside the German nation. Every German, for whom Christianity and *Volksthum* are sacred, must curtly

retort: *Never!*" Ibid. (emphasis in original). On the debate between Treitschke and Graetz, see Michael A. Meyer, "The
Great Debate on Antisemitism: Jewish Reaction to New Hos-
tility in Germany, 1879–1881," *Leo Baeck Institute Year Book*
11 (1966): 137–170, especially 154–159.

83. See note 75, above.

84. Cited in Bramsted, *Aristocracy and the Middle Classes
in Germany,* p. 147, n. 1.

85. Cited in Ernst Robert Curtius, *Kritische Essays* (Bern:
Francke, 1950), p. 153. Curtius, whose sympathies for French
literature disqualified him from membership in Stefan
George's elitist circle, was nonetheless close to the circle,
especially its Jewish members. See Kay E. Schiller, "The
Renaissance as Prototype and Remedy: The Transatlantic De-
velopment of German-Jewish Humanist Culture, 1918–1968"
(Ph.D. dissertation, University of Chicago, 1996), p. 46.

86. See Werner Mosse with the cooperation of A. Paucker,
ed., *Deutsches Judentum in Krieg und Revolution: 1916–1923*
(Tübingen: J. C. B. Mohr [Paul Siebeck], 1971), especially the
essay by Eva G. Reichmann, "Der Bewußtseinswandel der
deutschen Juden," pp. 511–612. George Mosse considers the
effects of the battlefront experience on German Jewish com-
batants in his "The Jews and the German War Experience,
1914–1918," *The Leo Baeck Memorial Lecture 21* (New York,
1977). On the vocal minority who decried the war, from across
the entire range of German Jewry, see Rivka Horwitz, "Voices
of Opposition to the First World War Among Jewish Thinkers," *Leo Baeck Institute Year Book* 38 (1988): 233–259.

87. See Egmont Zechlin, *Die deutsche Politik und die
Juden im Ersten Weltkrieg* (Göttingen: Vandenhoeck und
Ruprecht, 1969).

88. Hermann Cohen, "Ein Bekenntnis zur Judenfrage"
(1880), in *Der Berliner Antisemitismusstreit,* ed. Boehlich,
p. 126f.

89. See Hermann Cohen, *Jüdische Schriften,* ed. Bruno
Strauss (Berlin: C. A. Schwetschke und Sohn, 1924), 2:237–
301, 302–138.

90. Cf. "Staat und Nationalität sind nicht identisch. Staat
und Nation sind identisch." Hermann Cohen, "Deutschtum
und Judentum" (1915), in his *Jüdische Schriften,* p. 274. For
an extensive discussion of Cohen's views on these issues,

see Hartwig Wiedebach, *Die Bedeutung der Nationalität für Hermann Cohen* (Hildesheim: Georg Holms Verlag, 1997).

91. Cf. "The desire of the modern state to be a nation-state presents Judaism and the Jewish people with a dilemma. In this state, the Jews seem to form a 'state within a state' in that they constitute a distinct ethnic group *(Stamm)*. In the face of this modern dilemma, all liberal Jews *(freieren Juden)* in every state, without prior agreement, exclaim in self-defense: We do not want to form our own state, or, consequently, to be a separate nation. . . . *But we are and shall remain in principle a distinct ethnic group, a separate nationality.*" Hermann Cohen, "Antwort auf das offene Schreiben des Herrn Dr. Martin Buber an Hermann Cohen" (1916), in Cohen, *Jüdische Schriften*, 2:332 (emphasis added).

92. Cohen ascribes this development in his thought to an "insight" brought about by the world war. "For many decades one had questioned the viability of the Austrian state because it united within itself, it is claimed, so many nations. The terminology must now be changed. *The state unites within it not nations but nationalities.* It is the state that establishes and founds a nation, with which it equates itself. But this nation defined by the state can unite within it many nationalities. This historical insight must occur to every antisemite, and they ridicule only themselves, and their own nation-state, when they seek to deny us German Jews our membership in the German nation because of our continuing Jewish nationality." Hermann Cohen, "Religion und Zionismus" (1916), in Cohen, *Jüdische Schriften*, 2:322 (original emphasis).

93. On the Jewish Renaissance, which had its roots in the period immediately before the world war, and Rosenzweig's place in it, see Michael Brenner, *The Renaissance of Jewish Culture in Weimar Germany* (New Haven: Yale University Press, 1996), chap. 3.

94. Nahum N. Glatzer, *Franz Rosenzweig: His Life and Thought*, reprint (Cambridge: Hackett Publishing Co., 1998), pp. 23-31.

95. See Chapter 2.

96. Letter to Rudolf Hallo, dated the end of January 1923, in Franz Rosenzweig, *Briefe und Tagebücher* (2 vols.), ed. Rachel Rosenzweig and Edith Rosenzweig-Scheinmann with the assistance of Bernhard Casper, section 1 of *Der Mensch*

und sein Werk: Gesammelte Schriften (The Hague: Martinus Nijhoff, 1979), 2:888.

97. Heine, "Shakespeares Mädchen und Frauen," p. 124.

Chapter Two.
History and *Kultur:* The German-Jewish Perspective

1. Karl E. von Goebel, *Wilhelm Hofmeister* (Tübingen: J. C. B. Mohr [Paul Siebeck], 1924), p. 2. I wish to thank Dr. Heda Bondi Yudkis, Jerusalem, for bringing this vignette to my attention.

2. Nathaniel Pringsheim was the uncle of the mathematics professor Alfred Pringsheim (1850–1941), the father of Katja, the future wife of Thomas Mann.

3. Nigel Hamilton, *The Mann Brothers: The Lives of Heinrich and Thomas Mann* (New Haven: Yale University Press, 1979), p. 15.

4. See James C. Albisetti, *Schooling German Girls and Women: Secondary and Higher Education in the Nineteenth Century* (Princeton: Princeton University Press, 1988); and Phyllis Stock, *Better than Pearls: A History of Women's Education* (New York: G. P. Putnam's Sons, 1978), pp. 132–141. In the nineteenth century occasional exceptions were made for foreign-born women who had earned their matriculation abroad.

5. See Deborah Hertz, *Jewish High Society in Old Regime Berlin* (New Haven: Yale University Press, 1988).

6. For an extensive study of Jews and German Bildung, see George Mosse, *German Jews Beyond Judaism* (Bloomington: Indiana University Press, 1985), especially chap. 1. Also see Assmann, *Arbeit am nationalen Gedächtnis*, pp. 85–91. The overall significance of Bildung in the formation of German middle-class culture is discussed in ibid.; Walter H. Bruford, *The German Tradition of Self-Cultivation: "Bildung" from Humboldt to Thomas Mann* (Cambridge: Cambridge University Press, 1975); and Engelhardt, *"Bildungsbürgertum."* Also see Chapter 1, notes 22 and 23.

7. Mosse, *German Jews Beyond Judaism*, p. 7.

8. Hans Weil, *Die Entstehung des deutschen Bildungsprinzips* (Bonn: Cohen Verlag, 1930), p. 47.

9. See George Mosse, "Jewish Emancipation: Between *Bildung* and Respectability," pp. 1–16.

10. Mosse, *German Jews Beyond Judaism*, p. 11.

11. Scholem, "Jews and Germans," p. 79 (see Chapter 1, note 6).

12. German Jewry's abiding affection for Goethe is systematically examined in Wilfried Barner, *Von Rahel Varnhagen bis Friedrich Gundolf: Juden als deutsche Goethe-Verehrer* (Göttingen: Wallstein Verlag, 1992).

13. See Anton Nehamia Nobel, "Goethe, sein Verhältnis zu Religion und Religionen" (1921), *Bulletin des Leo Baeck Instituts* 12.48 (1969): 315–326.

14. Cited in Katz, "German Culture and the Jews" (see Chapter 1, note 8). For the source of the original German text, see the following note.

15. Friedrich Wilhelm Riemer, *Mittheilungen über Goethe aus mündlichen und schriftlichen, gedruckten und ungedruckten Quellen* (Berlin: Duncker und Humblot, 1841), 1:428.

16. Ibid.

17. Cited in Mosse, *German Jews Beyond Judaism*, p. 14.

18. Cohen, "Deutschtum und Judentum" (1915), pp. 278–80.

19. Cited in Jürgen Habermas, "The German Idealism of Jewish Philosophers," in Habermas, *Philosophical-Political Profiles*, trans. F. G. Lawrence (Cambridge: MIT Press, 1983), p. 25.

20. S. Friedländer, *Kant für Kinder: Fragelehrbuch zum sittlichen Unterricht* (Hanover: Paul Steegemann, 1924), p. 53.

21. Cited in Mosse, *German Jews Beyond Judaism*, p. 15.

22. See Elizabeth Petuchowski, "Zur Lessing-Rezeption in der deutsch-jüdischen Presse: Lessings 200. Geburtstag (22. Januar 1929)," *Lessing Yearbook* 14 (1982): 43–60. Also see Mosse, *German Jews Beyond Judaism*, p. 17.

23. See Robert Wistrich, "Fateful Trap: The German-Jewish Symbiosis," *Tikkun* 5.2 (March–April 1990): 34.

24. Theodore Wiener, "The German-Jewish Legacy: An Overstated Ideal," in *The German-Jewish Legacy in America, 1938–1988: From Bildung to the Bill of Rights*, ed. Abraham J. Peck (Detroit: Wayne State University Press, 1989), p. 153.

25. G. Steiner, "Some 'Meta-Rabbis,'" in *Next Year in Jeru-*

salem: Jews in the Twentieth Century, ed. Douglas Villiers (New York: Viking Press, 1976), p. 26.

26. Frederic V. Grunfeld, *Prophets Without Honor: A Background to Freud, Kafka, Einstein and Their World* (New York: Holt, Rinehart, and Winston, 1979).

27. For a more comprehensive review of the methodological issues entailed in the study of the alleged cultural preeminence of Jews in modern society, see my *Divided Passions: Jewish Intellectuals and the Experience of Modernity* (Detroit: Wayne State University Press, 1991), pp. 23–53.

28. See, e.g., Ernst van der Haag, *The Jewish Mystique* (New York: Stein and Day, 1969), pp. 13–25.

29. Peter Gay, "German Jews in German Culture, 1883–1914," *Midstream* (February 1975): 25, reprinted in Gay, *Freud, Jews and Other Germans: Masters and Victims in Modern Culture* (Oxford: Oxford University Press, 1978), p. 99.

30. See Arthur Ruppin, *Soziologie der Juden* (Berlin: Jüdischer Verlag, 1930), pp. 114–115.

31. See Mendes-Flohr and Reinharz, *Jew in the Modern World*, p. 708 (demographic table VIII).

32. Peter Pulzer, *The Rise of Political Anti-Semitism in Germany and Austria* (New York: Wiley, 1964), p. 11.

33. See Mendes-Flohr and Reinharz, *Jew in the Modern World*, p. 709 (demographic table IX).

34. See ibid., p. 710 (demographic table X). For a comprehensive study of the Jewish occupational structure in Germany, carried out on behalf of the Akademie der Wissenschaft des Judentums in Berlin, see Heinrich Silbergleit, *Die Bevölkerungs- und Berufsverhältnisse der Juden im Deutschen Reich* (Berlin: Akademie-Verlag, 1930).

35. Katz, "German Culture and the Jews," p. 91.

36. Pulzer, *Rise of Political Anti-Semitism*, p. 12.

37. *Encyclopedia Judaica* (1971), 13:970, s.v. "Prague."

38. Pulzer, *Rise of Political Anti-Semitism*, p. 12.

39. Albisetti, *Schooling German Women and Girls*, p. 216.

40. Marion Kaplan, "Tradition and Transition: The Acculturation, Assimilation and Integration of Jews in Imperial Germany—A Gender Analysis," *Leo Baeck Institute Year Book* 27 (1982): 26–29.

41. One could also mystify the Jews' embourgeoisement,

81. See "With Gershom Scholem: An Interview," in Scholem, *On Jews and Judaism in Crisis*, p. 1 f.

82. Bergmann to Buber, 19 September 1919, in *The Letters of Martin Buber*, ed. Nahum N. Glatzer and Paul Mendes-Flohr, trans. Richard Winston, Clara Winston, and Harry Zohn (New York: Schocken Books, 1992), p. 249 f. Bergmann's reference to a "Judaism of speeches" was a thinly veiled critique of Buber, the author of the famous *Drei Reden*, the speeches on Judaism (see notes 31 and 64, above). Cf. "And now [in the world war] since we have begun fighting for German *Kultur*, we feel more than ever what it means to us and how we are immersed in it with our whole being. I cannot imagine that our generation's artistically acquired relationship to biblical and hasidic Judaism, et cetera, will ever become so natural as our relationship to Fichte or to that man of European culture [Goethe] who showed us the way to humanism." Bergmann to Buber, 24 January 1917, in ibid., p. 251.

83. G. Reichmann, "Der Bewußtseinswandel der deutschen Juden," in *Deutsches Judentum in Krieg und Revolution, 1916–1923: Ein Sammelband*, ed. Werner Mosse in cooperation with Arnold Paucker (Tübingen: J. C. B. Mohr [Paul Siebeck], 1971), pp. 511–612; see also Zechlin, *Die deutsche Politik und die Juden*, pp. 516–567.

84. See Steven E. Aschheim, *Brothers and Strangers: The East European Jew in German and German Jewish Consciousness, 1800–1923* (Madison: University of Wisconsin Press, 1983), pp. 139–184, 215–252; Volkov, "Dynamics of Dissimilation," pp. 200–211; Jack Wertheimer, *Unwelcome Strangers: East European Jews in Imperial Germany* (New York: Oxford University Press, 1987), pp. 5–6, 56, 202–203; and Sander Gilman, "The Rediscovery of the Eastern Jews: German Jews in the East, 1890–1918," in Bronsen, *Jews and Germans from 1860 to 1930*, pp. 338–361.

85. Volkov, "Dynamics of Dissimilation," p. 211.

86. Blumenfeld's enduring fidelity to German culture is poignantly attested in his recently published correspondence with Hannah Arendt: "*. . . in keinem Besitz verwurzelt*": *Hannah Arendt–Kurt Blumenfeld—Die Korrespondenz*, ed. Ingeborg Nordhmann and Iris Pilling (Hamburg: Rotbuch Verlag, 1995), passim. Blumenfeld likewise acknowledged that his relation to German culture was dialectical: "Kampffähig

waren sie [die Zionisten] gegen den assimilierenden Einfluß
deutscher Kultur in dem Augenblick, in dem diese Kultur
ihnen zur Erkenntnis ihrer Sonderart die kritischen Mittel ge-
liefert hatte." Kurt Blumenfeld, "Deutscher Zionismus" (1912),
in Blumenfeld, *Zionistische Betrachtungen: Fünf Aufsätze*
(Berlin: Verein Jüdischer Studenten Maccabaea, 1916), p. 12.
Accordingly, as his lifelong friend Hannah Arendt reports, he
was wont to say, "Ich bin ein Zionist von Goethes Gnaden" (I
am a Zionist by the grace of Goethe), and he similarly argued
that "der Zionismus ist das Geschenk Deutschlands an die
Juden" (Zionism is the gift of Germany to the Jews). Hannah
Arendt to Karl Jaspers, 7 July 1952, in *Hannah Arendt-Karl
Jaspers Briefwechsel, 1926–1969*, ed. Lorre Saner and Hans
Saner (Munich: R. Piper Verlag, 1985), p. 234.

87. Bloch, "Symbol: Die Juden," p. 122.

88. Leo Strauss, preface to the English translation of his
Spinoza's Critique of Religion (New York: Schocken Books,
1965), p. 15.

89. Cohen, "Deutschtum und Judentum: Mit grundlegen-
den Betrachtungen über Staat und Internationalismus" (1915;
2d ed., 1916) and "Deutschtum und Judentum" (1916). The first
essay was published as a separate pamphlet, the second as an
article on "the inner peace of the German people." Both are
reprinted in *Hermann Cohens Jüdische Schriften*, ed. Bruno
Strauss with an introduction by Franz Rosenzweig (Berlin:
C. A. Schwetschke und Sohn, 1924), 1:237–301, 302–318.

90. Cohen, "Deutschtum und Judentum" (1916), p. 316;
Cohen, "The German and the Jewish Ethos II," in *Reason
and Hope: Selections from the Jewish Writings of Hermann
Cohen*, ed. and trans. Eva Jospe (New York: W. W. Norton and
Co., 1971), p. 187f.

91. Scholem, "On the Social Psychology of the Jews in
Germany," p. 22.

92. Steven S. Schwarzschild, " 'Germanism and Judaism'—
Hermann Cohen's Normative Paradigm of the German-Jewish
Symbiosis," in Bronsen, *Jews and Germans from 1860 to 1930*,
p. 132f.

93. Cohen, *Ethik des reinen Willens*, 2d ed. (Berlin: Bruno
Cassirer, 1907), p. 333f., cited in Schwarzschild, " 'Germanism
and Judaism,' " p. 141.

94. Cohen, "Deutschtum und Judentum" (1916), p. 317; Cohen, "German and Jewish Ethos II," p. 188.

95. Cohen, preface to the 2d edition of Cohen, *Ethik des reinen Willens*, p. viii, cited in Schwarzschild, "'Germanism and Judaism,'" p. 139.

96. Cohen, "Deutschtum und Judentum" (1915), p. 283. Since the English translation is an abridged version of the essay, I cite only the original German text when the given passages are not included in the English translation.

97. Ibid., p. 279.

98. Written at the outbreak of the world war, Lissauer's "Haßgesang gegen England" was for a time the most popular song in Germany. See Zechlin, *Die deutsche Politik und die Juden*, p. 97.

99. *Der Kunstwart*, 1 April 1912, p. 211.

100. Although the Judenzählung did not begin until October 1916, the public debate leading to the census had already been launched in August 1915, when Cohen published the first version of his essay "Deutschtum und Judentum." See Zechlin, *Die deutsche Politik und die Juden*, pp. 524 ff.

101. Cohen, "Deutschtum und Judentum" (1916), p. 317 f.; Cohen, "German and Jewish Ethos II," p. 188.

102. The actual reasons for establishing the government of the nascent German republic in Weimar had to do with political exigencies rather than sublime considerations of the city's symbolic association with the luminaries of German humanism. See Detlev J. K. Peukert, *The Weimar Republic: The Crisis of Classical Modernity*, trans. Richard Daveson (New York: Hill and Wang, 1987), p. 5 f.

103. Peter Gay, *Weimar Culture: The Outsider as Insider* (New York: Harper and Row, 1968).

104. Peter Gay, *Die Republik der Außenseiter: Geist und Kultur in der Weimarer Zeit, 1918–1933*, trans. Helmut Lindemann (Frankfurt: S. Fischer Verlag, 1970).

105. See Ismar Schorsch, "German Judaism: From Confession to Culture," in *Die Juden im nationalsozialistischen Deutschland, 1933–1943*, ed. Arnold Paucker (Tübingen: J. C. B. Mohr [Paul Siebeck], 1986), pp. 75–93; and Brenner, *Renaissance of Jewish Culture*, passim.

106. Hermann Cohen, *Die Religion der Vernunft aus den*

132   Notes to Pages 64–67

Quellen des Judentums, ed. B. Kellermann (Leipzig: Fock, 1919). The article *die* in the title of this first edition of the work was an inadvertent error and thus falsely reflected Cohen's conception of a "religion of reason." The misprint was corrected in the second edition of the work, published in 1929. The English translation follows the 1929 edition. See Hermann Cohen, *Religion of Reason out of the Sources of Judaism*, trans. Simon Kaplan (New York: Ungar, 1969).

107. On Rosenzweig's educational activities, see Rosenzweig, *On Jewish Learning* (see Chapter 2, note 69).

108. Rosenzweig, *Zweistromland: Kleinere Schriften* (see Chapter 2, note 73).

109. "Platons strahlende Welt und Kants erschauernde Tiefen / Strahlen Dir, Grosser, in eins, musisch erklagen sie Dir. / An der prophetischen Glut entbrannte die lodernde Fackel. / Sterbliches bargen wir hier. Lodere heller, O Glut." Cited in Nehemiah Nobel, *Thought and Halakhah: Collected Writings* (Hebrew), ed. Yeseyahu Aviad (Wolfsberg) (Jerusalem: Mosad Ha-Rav Kook, 1969), p. 45.

110. The allusion is to 1 Samuel 35:31.

111. The original Hebrew text is cited in Nobel, *Thought and Halakhah*, p. 45.

Chapter Four.
Franz Rosenzweig's Eulogy for German Jewry

1. See Brenner, *Renaissance of Jewish Culture* (see Chapter 1, note 93).

2. Leo Baeck, "Types of Jewish Understanding from Moses Mendelssohn to Franz Rosenzweig," *Judaism* (Spring 1969): 165.

3. See Franz Rosenzweig, *Hegel und der Staat*, 2 vols. (Munich, 1920; 2d ed., Aalen: Scientia Verlag, 1982).

4. The genealogical line to Rabbi Mordecai Jaffe is through Rosenzweig's great-grandfather, Samuel Meyer Ehrenberg. See Leopold Zunz, *Samuel Meyer Ehrenberg, Inspektor der Samsonschen Freischule zu Wolfenbüttel: Ein Denkmal für Angehörige und Freunde* (Braunschweig, 1854), p. 4. A photostat of Zunz's privately published essay was kindly given to me by the late Nahum N. Glatzer.

5. Rudolf Ehrenberg's relationship to the Maharal (Rabbi

Judah Löw ben Bezalel, c. 1525–1609) is through his great-grandfather David Gabriel Fischel, whose daughter Julie married Philipp Ehrenberg, Rudolf's grandfather. See Richard Ehrenberg, "Die Familien Ehrenberg und Fischel: Ein Beitrag zur Geschichte des Idealismus, den Geschwistern und den Nachkommen gewidmet." I wish to thank Rudolf Ehrenberg's granddaughter Professor Maria E. Ehrenberg for providing me with a copy of this unpublished memoir by her great-uncle.

6. See Zunz, *Samuel Meyer Ehrenberg*.

7. On Samuel Meyer Ehrenberg and the Samsonschule, see *Leopold and Adelheid Zunz: An Account in Letters*, ed. Nahum N. Glatzer (London: East and West Library, 1958), pp. xi–xiii; and R. Busch, *Lessings "Nathan" und jüdische Emanzipation im Lande Braunschweig* (Wolfenbüttel: 1981), pp. 104–114; and Zunz, *Samuel Meyer Ehrenberg*, pp. 20–44.

8. Zunz, *Samuel Meyer Ehrenberg*, p. 22.

9. Glatzer, *Franz Rosenzweig*, p. xii (see Chapter 1, note 94).

10. Victor Gabriel Ehrenberg, "Julie Ehrenberg, geb. Fischel (1827–1922): Erinnerung." Excerpts of this manuscript were transcribed by Maria E. Ehrenberg and included in a letter to me dated 12 March 1987.

11. Leopold Zunz, "Etwas über die rabbinische Literatur" (Berlin, 1818), translated in *Jew in the Modern World*, ed. Mendes-Flohr and Reinharz, pp. 221–230.

12. Ibid., p. 222.

13. Ibid.

14. Ibid.

15. Letter, Maria E. Ehrenberg to Paul Mendes-Flohr, dated 12 March 1987.

16. See Hans Ehrenberg, *Autobiography of a German Pastor*, trans. Geraint V. Jones (London: Student Christian Movement Press, 1946); and *Jenseits all unsres Wissens wohnt Gott: Hans Ehrenberg und Rudolf Ehrenberg zur Erinnerung*, ed. Rudolf Hermeier (Moers: Brendow Verlag, 1987).

17. Letter, Maria E. Ehrenberg to Paul Mendes-Flohr, 13 January 1988. Rudolf Ehrenberg's genealogical relationship to Luther was traced through Helene von Ihering's mother, Ida Christiana von Ihering, née Fröhlich (d.1868). Also see Maria Eugenie Ehrenberg, "Erinnerungen an meinen Vater Rudolf

Ehrenberg," in *Jenseits all unsres Wissens wohnt Gott,* ed. Hermeier, p. 74 f.

18. Interview with Hilla and Maria Ehrenberg, 12 March 1987, conducted on my behalf by Hans-Martin Dober and Christoph Lienkamp, at the home of Maria Ehrenberg, Würzburg, Germany.

19. I wish to thank Maria E. Ehrenberg for providing me with a photostat of the handwritten speech, which is among the Rudolf Ehrenberg papers that she administers.

20. Maria Ehrenberg, "Erinnerungen an meinen Vater," pp. 75–77.

21. Interview with Hilla and Maria Ehrenberg, 12 March 1987.

22. Zunz, *Samuel Meyer Ehrenberg,* p. 33 f.

23. Interview with Hilla and Maria Ehrenberg, 12 March 1987.

24. All citations from Rudolf Ehrenberg's speech at the Rosenzweig wedding are from the manuscript mentioned in note 19, above.

25. The occasion was the wedding of Victor Ehrenberg to Eva Sommer in April 1918. Rosenzweig's toast was published in Eva Ehrenberg, *Sehnsucht: Mein geliebtes Kind—Bekenntnisse und Erinnerungen* (Munich: Ner-Tamid Verlag, 1963), pp. 18–21.

26. Rudolf offered a quasi-ideological reason for the sudden change in the family tradition of the father using the Samuel Meyer Ehrenberg goblet to bless the son at his marriage. Maria Ehrenberg suggests that the original reason may have been rather mundane. In April 1919, when Victor Ehrenberg, Rudolf's and Franz's cousin, married in Frankfurt, his father could not make it to the wedding because of the revolutionary outbreaks then occurring in the country, so his cousin Franz offered the family wedding toast. Letter from Maria Ehrenberg to Paul Mendes-Flohr, dated 4 March 1988. Franz's father had died two years prior to his marriage, which explains why, at Franz's wedding, another family member, Rudolf Ehrenberg, made the blessing.

27. Rudolf Ehrenberg married Helene Frey in March 1914.

28. See Maria E. Ehrenberg, "Rudolf Ehrenbergs theoretische Biologie und Metabiologie: Hat der Dialog zwischen Rudolf Ehrenberg und Franz Rosenzweig zu ihrer Entste-

hung beigetragen?" in *Der Philosoph Franz Rosenzweig (1886–1929): Internationaler Kongreß — Kassel 1986*, ed. Wolfdietrich Schmied-Kowarzik, 2 vols. (Freiburg: Verlag Karl Alber, 1988), 1:159–163.

29. Rosenzweig's reflections on Lessing's *Nathan the Wise* were presented in two lectures that he gave to the Jewish community of Kassel in December 1919. See the notes outlining these lectures, "Lessings Nathan," pp. 449–453 (see Chapter 2, note 48).

30. Lessing, *Nathan the Wise*, act 2, scene 7.

31. Rosenzweig, "Lessings Nathan," p. 451.

32. Ibid., p. 450.

33. Ibid.

34. Ibid., p. 451.

35. Rosenzweig, "Vorspruch zu einer Mendelssohnfeier" (Autumn 1929), in his *Zweistromland*, p. 457. In another lecture, he refers to Mendelssohn as the "first Jewish human being [*Mensch*]." "Der jüdische Mensch" (Entwurf für die erste Vorlesungsreihe im Freien Jüdischen Lehrhaus von Oktober bis Dezember 1920), in ibid., p. 559.

36. Rosenzweig, "Der jüdische Mensch," p. 559.

37. Rosenzweig, "Lessings Nathan," p. 451.

38. Ibid.

39. Ibid., p. 452.

40. Rosenzweig, "Vorspruch zu einer Mendelssohnfeier," p. 457.

41. On Mendelssohn's philosophy of Judaism see Altmann, *Moses Mendelssohn*, pp. 514–552 (see Chapter 2, note 55).

42. Rosenzweig, "Der jüdische Mensch," p. 566.

43. Ibid.

44. Ibid.

45. Ibid., p. 567. In this respect, Rosenzweig regards German neo-Orthodox Judaism — according to whose teachings "Torah" was compatible with secular, humanistic culture — as essentially no different from Liberal or Reform Judaism.

46. See section 6, "German Humanism and Jewish Messianism," of the anthology of Cohen's Jewish writings: Hermann Cohen, *Reason and Hope*, trans., selected, and with an introduction by Eva Jospe (New York: W. W. Norton and Co., 1971), pp. 175–193.

47. Letter, Rosenzweig to his parents, 20 September 1917, in Rosenzweig, *Briefe und Tagebücher*, 1:443 f. (see Chapter 1, note 95).

48. Ibid., p. 444.

49. Ibid.

50. Ibid.

51. On Cohen's concept of Deutschtum as an idealistic construct employed to expose the limitations of the political reality of Germany, see Schwarzschild, " 'Germanism and Judaism,' " pp. 129–172.

52. Letter, Rosenzweig to his parents, 20 September 1917, p. 444.

53. Ibid., p. 445.

54. Cf. "One may discern [Cohen's fantasy of an affinity between Judaism and German culture] among all modern Jews, that is, insofar as they still wish to remain Jews." Letter, Rosenzweig to his parents, 20 September 1917, p. 442.

55. Ibid., p. 445.

56. Ibid.

57. Ibid., p. 443.

58. See Cohen's remarks in his debate with Martin Buber, "A Debate on Zionism and Messianism" (Summer 1916), in *Jew in the Modern World*, ed. Mendes-Flohr and Reinharz, pp. 571–577.

59. In spite of his respectful, even reverential regard for Cohen, Rosenzweig did not hesitate to criticize both the tone and presuppositions of Cohen's philosophy of Judaism. See, in particular, his "Einleitung in die Akademieausgabe der Jüdischen Schriften Hermann Cohens," in Rosenzweig, *Zweistromland*, pp. 177–223.

60. This criticism was first expressed obliquely in an essay entitled with the telling oxymoron "Atheistische Theologie." Written in 1914, it was published posthumously. For the German, see Rosenzweig, *Zweistromland*, pp. 699–712; for an English translation, see "Atheistic Theology," trans. Robert Goldy and H. Frederick Holoch, *Canadian Journal of Theology* 14.2 (1968): 79–88.

61. Rosenzweig, "Hermann Cohens Nachlaßwerk," in his *Zweistromland*, p. 231.

62. See Max Wiener, "The Concept of Mission in Tradi-

tional and Modern Judaism," *YIVO Annual of Jewish Science* 2–3 (1947–1948): 9–24.

63. Alexander Altmann, "Franz Rosenzweig on History," in *The Philosophy of Franz Rosenzweig*, ed. Paul Mendes-Flohr (Hanover: University Press of New England, 1988), pp. 124–137.

64. Rosenzweig, "Deutschtum und Judentum," in his *Zweistromland*, p. 169.

65. Ibid.

66. Ibid., p. 170.

67. Ibid.

68. See Paul Mendes-Flohr, "Rosenzweig and the Crisis of Historicism," in *Philosophy of Franz Rosenzweig*, ed. Mendes-Flohr, pp. 138–161.

69. See Franz Rosenzweig, *The Star of Redemption*, trans. William Hallo (New York: Holt, Reinhart, and Winston, 1970), part 3.

70. Ibid., pp. 328–335. Also see *Judaism Despite Christianity: The Letters on Christianity and Judaism Between Eugen Rosenstock-Huessy and Franz Rosenzweig*, ed. Eugen Rosenstock-Huessy (New York: Schocken Books, 1971).

71. For a discussion of Rosenzweig's view of history, see Altmann, "Franz Rosenzweig on History."

72. Ibid.

73. Franz Rosenzweig, "It Is Time," in *On Jewish Learning*, ed. Glatzer, p. 29 f.

74. Ibid., p. 28.

75. Ibid.

76. See Mendes-Flohr, "The Retrieval of Innocence and Tradition: Jewish Spiritual Renewal in an Age of Liberal Individualism," in *The Uses of Tradition: Jewish Continuity in the Modern Era*, ed. Jack Wertheimer (Cambridge: Harvard University Press, 1992), pp. 279–301.

77. Rosenzweig, "On Jewish Learning," cited in Glatzer, *Franz Rosenzweig: His Life and Thought*, p. 231 (see Chapter 1, note 94).

78. On Rosenzweig's Lehrhaus, see Glatzer, *On Jewish Learning*, p. 16 f.; Nahum N. Glatzer, "The Frankfort Lehrhaus," *Leo Baeck Institute Year Book* 1 (1956): 105–122.

79. Rosenzweig, "Deutschtum und Judentum," p. 170.

80. Ibid.

81. Rosenzweig, "Vorspruch zu einer Mendelssohnfeier," p. 457.

82. Letter, Franz Rosenzweig to Rudolf Hallo, end of January 1923, in Rosenzweig, *Briefe und Tagebücher*, 2:887 f.

Epilogue: Reflections on the Legacy of German Jewry

1. Robert Müller, "Phantasie," *Neue Rundschau* 2 (1916): 142.

2. Max Brod, "Unsere Literaten und die Gemeinschaft," *Der Jude* 1.7 (October 1916): 457.

3. Letter, Kafka to Felice Bauer, 7 October 1916, in Franz Kafka, *Briefe an Felice*, ed. Erich Heller and Jürgen Born (Frankfurt: S. Fischer Verlag, 1967), p. 720.

4. Rosenzweig's perspective, expounded in Chapter 4, may somewhat distort our appreciation of the fact that German Jews since the time of Moses Mendelssohn had struggled to maintain the dignity of Judaism while embracing German culture. By weaving their respective voices—and self-understanding—into one dialectical tale, by regarding them as mere dialectical moments leading to the Jewish Renaissance of his day, Rosenzweig undoubtedly obscured much of the historical nuance and interplay of their respective positions. He would certainly have acknowledged this, but he would also have retorted that a dialectical reading of history allows one to isolate and highlight broad trends.

5. Gay, *Weimar Culture* (see Chapter 3, note 103). Gay, "In Deutschland zu Hause: Die Juden der Weimarer Zeit," in *Die Juden im nationalsozialistischen Deutschland*, ed. Paucker, pp. 31–44.

6. See Jacob Toury, "Gab es ein Krisenbewußtsein unter den Juden während der 'Guten Jahre' der Weimarer Republik, 1924–1929?" in Toury, *Deutschlands Stiefkinder: Ausgewählte Aufsätze zur deutschen und deutsch-jüdischen Geschichte*, Schriftenreihe des Instituts für Deutsche Geschichte, Universität Tel Aviv (Gerlingen: Bleicher Verlag, 1997), pp. 191–214.

7. Kurt Blumenfeld, *Im Kampf um den Zionismus: Briefe aus fünf Jahrzehnten*, ed. Miriam Sambursky and Jochanan Ginat (Stuttgart: Deutsche Verlag-Anstalt, 1976), p. 269.

8. Toury, "Gab es ein Krisenbewußtsein?" p. 194 f.

9. Ibid., p. 206.

10. Scholem does not explicitly link the Holocaust to what he regards as the beguiling "illusion" of a Jewish-German dialogue, but his language certainly suggests such an association. While apologetically asserting that only deracinated, self-denigrating Jews—"Jews in flight from themselves"—are interested in a dialogue with Germans, Scholem speaks of a "dangerous dialectic." Scholem, "Once More: The German-Jewish Dialogue," p. 69 (see Chapter 1, note 6). Scholem characterizes this dialectic as being driven by an ironic logic that, from self-abnegating assimilation in the quest for emancipation, led, paradoxically, not to the Jews' integration into German society but to their "rejection." The illusion that assimilation would bring them acceptance "was one of the factors that retarded, disturbed, and eventually brought to a *gruesome end* the [dialectical] process." Further, "the refusal of so many German Jews to recognize the operation of such factors, and the dialectic to which they bear witness, is among the saddest discoveries made by today's reader of the discussions of those times." Scholem, "Jews and Germans," p. 77 (emphasis added; see Chapter 1, note 6). "[During the generations preceding the catastrophe], the German Jews . . . distinguished themselves by an astounding lack of critical insight into their own situation." Ibid., p. 89. Also see Scholem's autobiographical statement referring to his circle of friends in pre–World War I Berlin: "All of us shared the basic conviction that the great majority of our fellow Jews were living in a vacuum and, what was even more difficult and troubling to us, in a static self-deception in which they took their wishful thinking for reality—and entertained an illusion of German-Jewish harmony." Scholem, "On the Social Psychology of the Jews in Germany: 1900–1933," in Bronsen, *Jews and Germans from 1860 to 1930*, p. 26. The term "German-Jewish symbiosis" was apparently employed first by Buber, who introduced it in a lecture he gave in Jerusalem shortly after his emigration from Germany to Palestine in 1938. In this lecture, first published after the war, the symbiosis does not refer to a dialogue between Jews and Germans, but rather to the cross-fertilization of what Buber calls "the German and Jewish essence." Buber,

"Das Ende der deutsch-jüdischen Symbiose" (1939), in *Der Jude und sein Judentum: Gesammelte Aufsätze und Reden*, 2d ed. (Gerlingen: Lambert Schneider, 1992), pp. 629–632.

11. Jacob Katz, "War der Holocaust vorhersehbar?" in Katz, *Zwischen Messianismus und Zionismus: Zur jüdischen Sozialgeschichte* (Frankfurt: Jüdischer Verlag, 1993), pp. 202–232. An abridged version of this article was previously published in English under the title "Was the Holocaust Predictable?" in *Commentary Magazine* (May 1975): 41–48.

12. Katz, "War der Holocaust vorhersehbar?" p. 208.

13. See Mendes-Flohr, *Divided Passions: Jewish Intellectuals and the Experience of Modernity*, pp. 133–167 (see Chapter 2, note 27).

14. Landauer, "Sind das Ketzergedanken?"

15. See Norbert Altenhofer, "Tradition als Revolution: Gustav Landauers 'Geworden-Werden des Judentums,'" in Bronsen, *Jews and Germans from 1860 to 1930*, pp. 173–208.

16. In spite of his multicultural interests, Landauer nonetheless privileged German culture, if only by dint of the fact that his intellectual life was pursued in the German language, at the center of which were the canonical texts of German letters, especially those of Goethe and Hölderlin. See Bernd Witte, "Zwischen Haskala und Chassidut: Gustav Landauer im Kontext der deutsch-jüdischen Literatur- und Geistesgeschichte," in *Gustav Landauer im Gespräch: Symposium zum 125. Geburtstag*, ed. Hanna Delf and Gert Mattenklott (Tübingen: Max Niemeyer, 1997), pp. 25–42.

17. See Chapter 2.

18. See Brenner, *Renaissance of Jewish Culture*, passim.

19. On the Jüdische Kulturbund, see Brenner, *Renaissance of Jewish Culture*, pp. 213–220. Also see E. Geisel and H. M. Broder, eds., *Premiere und Pogrom: Der Jüdische Kulturbund, 1933–1941* (Berlin: Siedler Verlag, 1992); and Akademie der Künste zu Berlin, ed., *Geschlossene Vorstellung: Der Jüdische Kulturbund in Deutschland, 1933–1941* (Berlin: Edition Hentrich, 1992).

20. Elias Canetti, *The Human Province* (New York: Seabury Press, 1978), p. 51.

Index

Acculturation, 3. *See also* Assimilation, Jewish

Ahad Ha'am (Asher Ginzberg): critique of his cultural Zionism by Benjamin, 50–55, 125 n. 47; endorsement of his cultural Zionism by Ludwig Strauss, 50–51. *See also* Benjamin, Walter; Strauss, Ludwig

"And," the dialectics of, in the formation of a German-Jewish identity, 21, 60, 75–88, 90

Antisemitism: alleged Jewish talent for commerce and capitalism, 116 n. 41; and Fontane, 8; Jewish responses to, 102 n. 27; and *Kunstwart* debate, 122 n. 10. *See also* Emancipation, Jewish; World War I, Hitler, Adolf; Holocaust; National Socialism; Nazis; "State within a state"

Arendt, Hannah, xi, 130 n. 86

Art, Jews as collectors of, 119 n. 59. *See also* Museums

Asher, Saul: response to Fichte's attack on the Jews, 108 n. 64

Assimilation, Jewish, 3, 18–20, 57–59, 82, 98 n. 7. *See also* Dissimilation

Assmann, Aleida: on the concept of *Bildung*, 8–12; and "the work of memory" incumbent on postwar Germany, 103 n. 34

Atheistic theology, Rosenzweig's critique of, 136 n. 60

Auerbach, Berthold, 13

Aufklärer, 13, 27

Aufklärung, 13, 34, 45. *See also* Enlightenment

Auschwitz, 92, 98 n. 7

Avenarius, Ferdinand, 46–47. See also *Kunstwart* debate

Babylonia. See *Zweistromland*

Babylonian Talmud, 23

Bach, Johann Sebastian, 84

Baeck, Leo, 44, 66

Barbarossa, myth of: and German identity, 110 n. 75; Jews' difficulty in identifying with, 17. *See also* Frederick I

Beethoven, Ludwig van, 31

Benjamin, Walter: on bifurcated soul of the German Jew, 51; correspondence with Ludwig Strauss, 20,

Hebrew language, 51. *See also*
Strauss, Ludwig
Hegel, G. W. F., 31, 39, 45,
60, 66, 82. *See also* Cohen,
Hermann; Rosenzweig,
Franz
Heine, Heinrich: on cosmopolitan proclivities of Jews,
110 n. 76; on elective affinity between Jews and
Germans, 23; *Leaves from
the Memoirs of Herr von
Schnabelewopski*, 1–2;
prophecy of a New Jeru-
salem, 23; on writing of
history, 1–2
Herder, J. G.: on Barbarossa
myth, 17, 110 n. 75; con-
ception of *Bildung*, 9–10,
26, 104 n. 37; and notion of
the state, 15–16; theory of
palingenesis, 110 n. 75. See
also *Volksnation*
Herzl, Theodor, 56, 126 n. 48
History: comparison of Jewish,
French, and German sense
of, 17–18, 25–44 passim;
Lessing's and Mendels-
sohn's contrasting views
of history, 37–39, 118 n. 5;
Rosenzweig on relation of
Judaism to history and culture, 82–83. *See also* Heine,
Heinrich; Rosenzweig,
Franz; Treitschke, Heinrich
von
Hitler, Adolf, 24, 42, 66, 92
Hoffmanstahl, Hugo von, 46
Hoffmeister, Wilhelm, 25
Hölderlin, Friedrich: Ludwig
Strauss's dissertation on,
55–56; mentioned, 140 n. 16
Holocaust, German-Jewish
history from the perspective

of, 2, 31, 88, 91–95, 139 n. 10.
See also Auschwitz; Hitler,
Adolf; Scholem, Gershom
Humboldt, Wilhelm von, 10,
14, 17, 25

Ihering, Helene von, 70

Jacob, Benno, 3
Jaffe, Mordecai, 67
Jefferson, Thomas: politi-
cal theory anticipated by
Mendelssohn, 109 n. 68
Jewish artists and Jewish
Renaissance, 57–58. *See
also* Jewish Renaissance in
Germany
Jewish Renaissance in Ger-
many: artists of, 57–58;
Bergmann's critique of, 58,
129 n. 82; Buber and, 93–94,
128 n. 78; Ludwig Strauss
on, 50; and postassimilation,
63; in post–First World War
period, 22, 63–67; Rosen-
zweig on, 22, 66–67, 86–87,
90, 93–94, 113 n. 93; and
Zionism, 57. See also *Jude,
Der*; New Babylon
Jewish studies, modern, 68.
See also *Wissenschaft des
Judentums*
Jewry, East European, 52, 58,
126 n. 58
Jost, Isaac Marcus, 68
Judaism: Liberal, 77, 80–81;
Orthodox, 20, 135 n. 45;
Reform, 20, 77. *See also*
Esoteric Judaism
"Judaism of Speeches." *See*
Bergmann, Shmuel Hugo
Jude, Der, 22, 56
Judenzählung (Jewish census),
62, 131 n. 100